COUNSELING
ADOLESCENT GIRLS

COUNSELING ADOLESCENT GIRLS

PATRICIA H. DAVIS

FORTRESS PRESS   MINNEAPOLIS

For Sarah, my daughter and friend

COUNSELING ADOLESCENT GIRLS

Scripture quotations unless otherwise noted are from the Revised Standard Version of the Bible copyright © 1946, 1952, and 1971 or the New Revised Standard Version Bible © 1989 by the Division of Christian Education of the National Council of Churches of Christ in the United States of America. Used with permission.

Cover photo © Skjold

ISBN 0-8006-2905-1

The paper used in this publication meets the minimum requirements of American National Standard for Information Sciences—Permanence of Paper for Printed Library Materials, ANSI Z329.48-1984. ∞™

Manufactured in the U.S.A.   AF 1-2905

00   99   98   97   96   1   2   3   4   5   6   7   8   9   10

CONTENTS

FOREWORD

Ours is a society where countless women and men are searching for more wholeness—liberating gender definitions that can enable both sexes to move toward the goal of Christian lifestyles—life in all its fullness. In this cultural context, it is fortunate that this book makes a much needed contribution to the pastoral care and counseling literature. It does so by helping fill a gap in pastoral resources—pastorally oriented books focusing specifically on the complex care giving issues involved in working with girls who are struggling with the confusion and conflicts of "adolescing" in today's society.

Patricia Davis's insights and methods throw helpful light on how caregivers can respond therapeutically to girls who are severely wounded by problems such as incest, dating violence, eating disorders, depression, and sexual issues. But, a major strength of this book is that the author lays a firm foundation for counseling such deeply wounded girls by showing how *all* adolescent girls are at risk of being wounded to some degree in our sexist culture. Many girls who may not seem to be severely disturbed need help because of the well-documented ways in which their self-esteem and sense of inner strength is diminished early in adolescence by our society. Adolescent boys often stumble and fall with an obvious crash on today's rocky road to male adulthood. But, as Patricia Davis points out, the developmental road that girls walk has even greater risks for them, with huge gender-specific perils and dangerous detours. Girls are even more vulnerable than boys to being exploited, manipulated, and subjected to physical and sexual abuse.

This book aims at enabling caregivers to understand these hazards in our culture, our families, and our churches, and thereby "to see girls in a new way." Those who acquire this new way of seeing girls will be much better equipped to guide them in coping constructively with the perils and avoiding the potentially disastrous detours on their teen-to-adult passage. These caregivers will understand more fully the three interacting levels of all the concerns, crises, and symptoms that girls bring to ministers and youth leaders—the cultural, the family, and the personal.

The convincing evidence presented by the author makes it clear that clergy and congregations often contribute unwittingly but in major ways to the disempowering, self-devaluing, and distorted spirituality of girls. Religious leaders, lay and professional, who have their consciousness raised about the issues that this book explores and illuminates can better utilize the opportunities they have to help heal but also to prevent such damage to girls' sense of full selfhood. In addition, they also can help boys understand and change the ways their attitudes and behavior contribute to both girls' problems and their own. Such church leaders can take the initiative in the needed remedial education of their church communities concerning the destructive impact of sexist attitudes, policies, and behavior on girls and also on boys.

This book will, I predict, be read with profit by pastoral caregivers of both genders who work with adolescent girls and their families. Its eye-opening insights will also be useful for mothers and fathers seeking to understand and to help their teenage girls develop their fullest gifts in these turbulent times of transition in gender identities. The book also will be of value to youth counselors and teachers in secular as well as church-related settings. It will highlight the need of girls to have more opportunities to relate to strong, caring, competent women as role models and mentors. These certainly should include clergywomen, female pastoral counselors, youth workers, and teachers. The book has the potential of enabling these crucial givers of care to become more aware of how the future well-being of women and the families many of them will co-create, depend on providing healing experiences that enable girls to gain a fuller awareness of their Creator-given worth and strength.

On a professional level, I read Patricia Davis's book with the eyes of an appreciative pastoral caregiver. But on a personal level, I read it with the eyes of a father of an adult daughter and the grandfather of two granddaughters, one still a young child and the other an adolescent. For both professional and personal reasons, I am thankful that this book is now available as a resource for all who care with conviction about seeking to make all caregiving more wholeness-making for all females, our sisters in the human family.

HOWARD CLINEBELL

ACKNOWLEDGMENTS

Many people have contributed to this book in various ways. First, I thank Perkins School of Theology for its generosity in giving me a research leave and a Faculty Outreach Grant to complete this manuscript. I am also grateful for Dr. Robert A. Armour and the Sam Taylor Fellowship Fund of the Board of Higher Education and Ministry of the United Methodist Church for a grant to complete the research involved in chapter 3, Girls' Spirituality.

Several people were involved in helping me to find girls who would be willing to talk to me about their spirituality. I am especially grateful to Christi Shdeed of the Parish Day School of the Episcopal Church of the Transfiguration in Dallas, the Rev. Sheron C. Patterson of Crest-Moore King United Methodist Church of Oak Cliff, Daniel Kincaid of Groton School, Judith Reedy, the Rev. David Cox and Marlene Dickinson of the Church at the Crossing in Indianapolis, and the Rev. Robert Cannon at Epworth United Methodist Church in Indianapolis.

Thanks to Cynthia Thompson who helped bring this project to completion. Carol Adams was a wonderful coach. Marguerite Moss gave extremely helpful insights regarding women's spirituality. Christie Neuger, Howard Clinebell, and Charlotte Ellen read an early manuscript and gave invaluable feedback, and Valerie Bridgeman Davis was always there with a prayer, an uncannily timed phone call, and a poem. Lisa Diller shared encouragement and stories. Pat Elia, Lou Ginsburg, Ernie Campbell, and the Cape May County, New Jersey, Youth and Family Services Crisis Intervention Unit allowed me to work on the "front lines" with them, and shared their incomparable wisdom and "cool."

Many thanks to my father, Bill Davis, who recruited the recruiters in Indianapolis; to the other "Davis women" (Margaret, Susan, Barbara, Terri, Jacqueline, and Sarah) and to Marion Howery for their strength; and to Tom Davis for sharing his expertise and insight. I owe my husband, Steve Howery, a huge debt for his wisdom, care, patience, and support. Tom, thanks for your sense of humor and for loaning me your CD player.

Finally, my deepest thanks to the many wonderful girls who took part in my study. You shared sacred parts of your life with me, and consistently amazed me with your creativity, faith, insight, and clear vision. And to Sarah—this is for you.

RECOGNIZING

     Just a Flash
Still
     Someone inside peeked
         from behind the pain
and
     you knew her—
     It was not the smile,
         nor the way she held her head sideways;
     It was not the flow of her dress,
         nor the way her hair resisted the wind;
     Just a Flash
Still
     she peeked out and you said, "Hi."

—Valerie J. Bridgeman Davis

INTRODUCTION

*I can envision my daughter as a bright, capable, and success-
ful young adult, but I'm afraid to think of her as a teenager.*
—Mother of an eight-year-old

*Let's face it, we're afraid of our children these days. We're
scared to death of them.*
—Alex Williams, State District Attorney
for Prince George's County, MD

I feel stupid and contagious.
—Kurt Cobain (1967–1994)

Adolescence, the stage of life between the beginning of puberty and the
assumption of full adult responsibilities (Fuhrmann 1990), is a tumul-
tuous and vulnerable time for everyone who passes through it. Working
with adolescents has never been an easy task; youth ministries are notoriously hard work. In their positions youth leaders more and more
frequently face incredibly complicated situations with teens, their parents, and the community. They are called upon to be theologians, social
workers, recreation directors, program organizers, and personal counselors. Often they labor in environments which downplay the importance of their work and of the youth with whom they work.

Today, there is disturbing agreement in many quarters that adolescents
are, in a sense, lost causes—the media describe a generation (Generation
X, thirteeners) without hope, without ambition, and without faith. Adolescents are seen as not reliable; their ideas, opinions, viewpoints, and
knowledge are not solicited. When they are listened to, it is often to gain
access to the large amounts of income some have at their disposal.

Even those elements of our culture that claim to represent and stand for
adolescents cynically exploit them. In the *New York Times* Business Section

an advertisement by MTV (the self-proclaimed voice of adolescents) reveals its exploitation of its own constituents: It consists of a photograph of an obviously bored young man, seated in a comfortable chair with a remote control in his hand. The caption: "Buy this [kid] and get all his friends absolutely free. . . . What he eats, his friends eat. What he wears, they wear. What he likes, they like. And what he's never heard of . . . well . . . you get the idea." Thus MTV offers up its viewers to Madison Avenue—"*Buy* this kid!" (*New York Times*, 6/15/93, C14).

And what is true regarding the exploitation and devaluing of adolescents in general is especially true for young women. As many youth leaders will attest, adolescent girls are in many ways more vulnerable to psychological and physical injury at this time than their male counterparts. Girls are at risk in their families, in their culture, and in the church today. They are at risk for sexual and physical abuse; they are at risk for developing eating disorders; they are at risk for depression and suicide; they are at risk for disruptions in their relationships with parents and family; they are at risk for deadly sexually transmitted diseases and unplanned pregnancy; they are at risk for alcohol and drug abuse; and, perhaps most importantly, they are at risk for losing a sense of their own power, value, and importance in the universe.

Developmental psychologists who are sensitive to the differences between girls and boys as they enter puberty and young adulthood are discovering that this time is often particularly difficult for the girls. Researchers find that in early adolescence especially, girls are prone to depression and to losing hold of their precious newly emerging identities. This is not surprising in a culture that misunderstands and ignores their perceptions and visions, but is eager to exploit them for financial and other unethical gain (Fine, Mortimer, and Roberts, 1990).

The primary purpose of this book is to be an "outsiders' " guide to the often confusing, often dangerous, and often surprisingly delightful world of the adolescent girl. As will become clear, this volume does not intend to prepare pastors or lay youth workers to become *therapists* for girls. Instead, one of its aims is to prepare those who work most closely with young women in the church to recognize and be sensitive to various problems and conditions that they will encounter in the girls. Youth pastors and workers will often be the only adults in whom young women will confide; these adults can become—if they have eyes to see and willingness to act—incredibly important bridges to professional treatment and help for girls at risk.

A second purpose of this book is to help those who work with girls to see them in a new way. I hope the book will assist caregivers in uncovering the positive aspects of what may seem to be negative behaviors in some girls. These behaviors can often be seen as resistance to those forces (in the culture, their families, their peer groups, or their churches) that attempt to exploit and undermine the girls. Our job as caregivers is not to quash healthy resistance to exploitation (even when it looks like misbehavior, acting out, or is potentially dangerous), but to make sure that the resistance is as effective and minimally self-destructive as possible. Part of this process is to become aware, for ourselves, of those elements in our culture, families, and churches that are dangerous for girls.

This coming-to-awareness on the part of the caregiver often involves a painful process of self-discovery. But before those of us who work with adolescent girls will be able to be effective, we need to take a hard look at the culture in which they live, and to recall and to reflect upon our own experiences of adolescence.

One of the underlying principles of the book is that all problems are multilayered. In every instance the concerns, crises, and symptoms that girls bring to ministers and youth leaders are rooted in at least three levels of experience: the cultural, the family, and the personal. This book, in very brief form, is aimed at helping caregivers to begin to analyze all three levels. A problem resolved at only one or two levels will certainly resurface again and again—perhaps in different forms, on a different level. Most caregivers do not need to be told that most problems, especially those primarily rooted in the culture, will probably never be fully resolved. Experienced ministers know how carefully to balance expectations for positive outcomes with realism about the limitations of the context in which they function. In all probability, working with girls will break our hearts on a regular basis; it may also give us renewed faith in the human spirit.

Chapter One describes girls in two very specific cultural contexts: their early lives in their families, and their lives in the educational system, especially in high school. It describes the life experience of girls as they are trained to be nurturers and caregivers, and to be satisfied with life in the private world of the family home. This training surprisingly has remained constant even in families and school systems which have made attempts to change gender-role stereotyping.

Chapter Two describes girls' psychological journey from childhood to adulthood using the theories of Erik Erikson and Carol Gilligan. Erikson's work provides a key to understanding the work a girl must do to achieve an identity independent of her friends and her family. Gilligan's work shows that in addition to gaining independence a girl must also learn how to remain in relationship with those she loves and about whom she cares.

Chapter Three focuses on forty-four girls' responses to a spirituality questionnaire which was designed and administered for this volume. The girls' answers show deep sensitivity to spiritual issues in their lives, and amazing creativity in solving the theological problem of imaging God. The responses also show the ways in which socialization affects girls' ideas of who God is; many struggled with the idea that God is male, but they are female. Pastoral caregivers are encouraged to take girls' theological issues seriously, and to look closely at the implications of what at first may seem to be simple questions.

Chapter Four discusses girls' relationships in their families, both to their individual parents and to their families as a whole. Communication problems and role rigidity, two of the most common family problems which pastoral caregivers will encounter in adolescents, are described and suggestions are given for ways caregivers can assist families to deal with them.

Chapter Five focuses on the difficult issue of violence against girls by looking at the problems of incest and dating violence. Instructions are given for handling a girl's disclosure that she is being abused by a family member. Ways of creating safe environments for girls are described, and issues relating to the caregiver's own sexuality are discussed.

Chapter Six is an overview of "first aid" treatment for three major problems which adolescent girls may bring to a pastoral caregiver: eating disorders, depression, and sexual problems. This chapter outlines symptoms and referral strategies for each of these issues, and makes suggestions for pastoral interventions if they are necessary.

A caveat for readers of this book: We have all observed that there is no *one* adolescent character. Indeed, one of the characteristics of adolescence is a constant revising of and testing of personal goals, aims, likes, dislikes, and even personality, on an almost daily basis. It is obvious also that there is no one adolescent *girl*, with one stereotypical set of problems and needs to analyze or describe. No two girls will be affected the same way by any situation, cultural phenomenon, or family configuration.

By necessity this book deals with general issues and problems. It also, however, attempts to introduce readers to individual girls of different ages, ethnicities, religious backgrounds, and geographical locations through case studies, interviews, responses to the spirituality questionnaire, and journal entries.

One of the disciplines of writing this book was to remember that pastoral care for girls is not about statistics but rather about individuals and specific communities. One of the disciplines of reading this book will be the effort every reader needs to make to translate this material into his or her own situation and community of faith. The girls you work with will not be personally represented here; I hope, however, the issues raised and situations described will be recognizable. We need to learn to listen carefully; the girls have much they want to tell us!

1

STARTING FROM BEHIND

Observations about adolescence always *imply comments on society, on the sexes, [and] on the structures by which we order experience.* . . .

—Patricia Myers Spacks, *The Adolescent Idea*

Why should we as caregivers separate the needs of adolescent girls from those of adolescent boys? Why focus specifically on girls? One of the first issues we must deal with is that of gender difference. Indeed, I encountered this question frequently when I spoke with adolescents about the project. Girls sometimes felt surprised and singled out; boys felt ignored and neglected.

The answer to the question of gender is both practical and philosophical: adolescent girls live in a different world than their male peers. To put it more precisely: adolescent girls have a different experience of the world they share with adolescent boys. Obviously, they experience the world through different bodies; their bodies grow and change in different ways and at different rates. But they also live in different social worlds than their male counterparts. As will be shown, girls live in a world established on masculine or *androcentric* norms, designed to enhance certain masculine experience and power and to devalue their own. The hard truth is, unless a girl's life closely resembles that of the most privileged males around her, she will not be able to achieve as much personally or professionally as they do. And, indeed, without the permission of these privileged males, she will achieve relatively little. As Adrienne Rich has argued: "[As a woman] whatever my status of situation, my derived economic class, or my sexual preference . . . I have access only to so much of privilege or influence as the patriarchy is willing to accede to me and only for so long as I pay the price for male approval (1986, 58).

We who work with adolescent girls will misunderstand them if we do not take seriously the "facts of life" for women and girls in this culture as reflected in the brief fact list below:

- Over 500,000 girls and women were the victims of rape, attempted rape, other sexual assault, or threats each year in 1992 and 1993 (U.S. Department of Justice 1995).
- 44 percent of women in this country have been the victim of rape or attempted rape (Russell and Howell, 1983).
- 38 percent of all girls have been the victim of childhood sexual abuse before the age of 18 (Russell 1986).
- Women are six times more likely than men to be the victims of a violent crime committed by an intimate (relative or acquaintance) (Harlow 1991).
- 65 percent of girls have been grabbed, touched, or pinched in a sexual way in high school (American Association of University Women 1993).
- Three out of five of the 7.7 million single mothers in the United States live at or near the poverty level with a median annual income of $9,353 ("Women Work!" 1994).

The central fact of every North American adolescent girl's life (whether she realizes it or is mystified by it) is this: she is indeed a stranger in a strange land. She inhabits a world that presents itself as safe, but which will, in actuality, probably ignore, devalue, or hurt her. Statistically, she will be no safer when she becomes a woman.

The implications of this fact for girls and for those who work with them are enormous. It must be taken into account in every interaction we have with girls whether we ourselves are men or women. Our temptation—conscious or not—to agree with the culture about girls' low value is immense. For, as we know, even the very word "adolescence" has a negative value in our culture. To say someone is "adolescent," or "acting like an adolescent" is to dismiss their feelings, to minimize their pain, and to disregard their thoughts. When this negative feeling about "adolescence" is compounded by our own cultural negativity about "female" we must be very aware of our own (sometimes hidden) tendencies to devalue the experience of those girls with whom we work.

A good test of this propensity to overlook girls' vision and insight is to remember reactions to the furor over President Jimmy Carter's reference to talking with his then teenaged daughter, Amy, regarding the issue of nuclear nonproliferation. President Carter was derided as someone who had no sense—to ask a *girl* about an important issue such as this. Would there have been a similar reaction to his consulting one of his adolescent *sons*?[1]

This chapter will focus on two aspects of girls' destructive relationship with their culture, and the psychological results of these. The first has to do with girls' primary socialization in their families. Girls' early family experience and Western cultural expectations about mothering and fathering have deep and lasting implications for the emotional lives of both girls and boys. The second is girls' secondary socialization in the institution with the most power and influence for all children in our culture—the school. The classroom is one of most important places to learn whether or not one can achieve and do the work that the social world expects. Unfortunately, according to recent American Association of University Women research, because of differential treatment of girls and boys, the classroom is one of the first places that girls begin to learn to doubt their own worth and experience.

EARLY FAMILY LIFE

In Euro-American culture women are given the role of primary caregivers. Because of this role, women's central concerns have become how to care for self and others and how to be in relationship with others. In most families (even most of those that consider themselves egalitarian) women are in charge of those activities which bring people together and foster family relationships. Women care for the children and the sick, send birthday cards, organize holidays, decorate the home, and plan outings for the family. Men in families tend to be more in charge of house maintenance and family business matters (Hochschild 1989). These nurturing concerns of women are not inborn, genetic, or the function of role-training alone, but rather are the result of cultural training and psychological processes.

If we wonder whether these role structures are still very much in place today, we can, for example, do quick reviews of toy catalogues and television commercials aimed at children, which are still mostly segregated between boys' and girls' products. Boys are mostly offered action-adventure toys, while girls are offered dolls, doll houses, princess costumes, and toy home appliances.

Nancy Chodorow, a sociologist, has argued that a girl's desire to be maternal and nurturing comes out of her very early attachment to her mother or maternal figure. Because women are more closely associated with the primary maternal role, they tend to be close to home and to the children; fathers tend to carry on the more public family roles and are thus more remote from the family. This parental role configuration influences the ways in which children of both genders experience early childhood. For boys the break from the close mother and identification with the remote father, which normally take place around ages three and four, are fairly complete. Most boys learn to be separate, and they form strong individual identities. For most girls the process is more complex, and the break from their mothers is never total. Rather, even when girls begin to develop sexual attraction to others outside the family, they also remain connected with their mothers.

Mothers, for their part, experience their sons as male opposites, but experience their daughters as less distinct individuals and more continuous with themselves. Boys, being directed away from their mothers and their mothers' concerns and toward their fathers, who are more remote from families, tend to develop clear senses of autonomy and individuation. Girls, in contrast, who remain in closer relationship with their mothers, tend to have weaker ego boundaries—the distinction between self and other is not so clear. As a result they develop much more refined capacities for empathy. Chodorow's point is that for girls empathy, nurture and relationship maintenance are by-products of both the social situation, which gives mothers the primary caretaking/nurturing role, and their own early childhood experiences within that social structure (Chodorow 1978).

This development is not a neutral thing for women and girls, however, because of the different values our culture places on individuality and relationship. The rugged individuality developed in boys equips them to function in the public sphere where most cultural power inheres. The nurturing ability developed in girls, preparing them for their female domestic nurturing roles, is not valued as highly in the world of work and social power.

Men dominate institutions which legislate and in other ways control both the public and private arenas. Men's power includes the power to name "reality"—and it is the power which makes girls feel as if their experience (and the experience of their mothers) is not real or is not valued. Powerful men are seen as the standard for normality; to differ from this standard is to be sick and deficient.

GIRLS' SOCIALIZATION IN THE CLASSROOM

For women this male construction of reality is probably nowhere clearer than in the world of paid employment. Women consistently earn lower wages than men. They are discriminated against in multiple ways because of their childbearing and childrearing responsibilities. They are promoted less than men, and to less high positions. They are traditionally assigned to careers and positions that are directed toward care and nurture (e.g., teachers and counselors) and that are subordinate to their male counterparts (e.g., nurse, secretary, flight attendant, administrative assistant, paralegal) (Bem 1993).

For girls the male construction of reality is most clearly seen in the world of school. Statistics relating to girls' achievement in the classroom are eye-opening and disturbing:

- In the early grades girls are ahead of or equal to boys on almost every standardized measure of achievement and psychological wellbeing. By the time they graduate from high school or college, they have fallen behind.
- In high school, girls score lower on the SAT and ACT tests, which are critical for college admission. The greatest gender gap is in the crucial areas of science and math.
- Girls score far lower on College Board Achievement tests, which are required by most of the highly selective colleges.
- Boys are much more likely to be awarded state and national scholarships.
- Women score lower on all sections of the Graduate Record Exam, which is necessary to enter many graduate programs, the GMAT for business school, the LSAT for law school, and the MCAT for medical school (Sadker and Sadker 1994, 13–14).

Schools, especially high schools, do much more than just impart knowledge to young adults. The secondary school not only teaches math, science, language, and literature "lessons" but also continues and intensifies the character-forming function of the primary schools through such activities as sports, music, drama, peer groups and clubs, dances and proms, etc., which have much more to do with shaping the person than with "knowledge" transmission. For girls this integration of knowledge and life can be a very difficult thing, because both positive and negative influences are highlighted and consolidated. The school itself, perhaps unintentionally, often contributes much more to the negative aspect of learning for girls; secondary school education is far from gender neutral. It is often more tailored to the needs and achievement of male students.

Secondary education's bias toward males can be demonstrated in at least two different ways which will be discussed below. First, and most importantly, classrooms tend to render female students invisible, silent, and depressed. Second, when girls receive academic and vocational guidance in high school, they are often steered toward traditionally female occupations.

Invisible Girls in the Classroom

Research spanning the last twenty years has shown that from the very early grades girls are likely to be invisible members of their classrooms (American Association of University Women 1992, 68). Teachers tend to interact with boys much more often than with girls; they ask boys more helpful questions, and give them better feedback than their female peers (Sadker and Sadker 1994, 1).

For example, in one study of elementary and middle school classrooms, boys called out answers eight times more often than girls. These boys tended to be listened to; girls who attempted to call out tended to be corrected and told such things as, "Please raise your hand if you want to speak" (Sadker and Sadker 1981, 33–38). Studies done on upper level classes in math and science (traditionally seen as male areas) have shown that "boys are the object of more disciplinary remarks but also of more jokes, personal statements, encouragement, and praise" than girls (Entwistle 1990, 207). Boys and their learning and social needs tend to be taken seriously in the classroom; girls are often assumed to have fewer needs and less to offer. Many girls can never overcome this indifference or hostility and do not achieve what, in more favorable circumstances, might be hoped for or expected of them.

Becca, a thirteen-year-old Anglo girl, interviewed about her school experience, perceptively describes her invisibility and her resultant reluctance to speak. She talks about not responding to questions in class "unless I'm really, really sure of an answer and sometimes not even then." She complains that the teachers make her feel "invisible" when she does try to participate. After trying, but not being able to get her English teacher's attention one day she observed, "You know how some people have charisma? I have, like, *negative* charisma. I feel like I can be talking and people can be looking right at me and they don't even see me." Her invisibility, rendered by insensitive teachers, has drastic effects on her self-esteem and on her school performance. The interviewer writes that Becca eventually withdraws from her schoolwork as a defense against the neglect and pain (Orenstein 1994, 24).

Like Becca, many girls choose to be silent rather than to risk the shame and humiliation of being invisible. While boys are being attended to, taught, and corrected—honing their own powers of speech and thought—girls lose ground daily.

It is not, however, only in verbal classroom interaction that girls tend to lose out. The American Association of University Women's recent report points out that girls lose out in another important respect: women's and girls' lives and achievements are not represented in the formal curriculum. Despite research that clearly shows the positive effects of including books by women authors in high school English class required reading lists, a 1989 study shows that there has been little change in overall gender balance of authors from lists of 80 years ago (AAUW 1993, 64). Despite the stated intentions of many textbook publishers to delete sexism in their materials, very little progress has been made in that direction; research on high school social studies texts has shown that important women are rarely introduced to students, nor are their contributions discussed (AAUW 1993, 64).

In a study conducted in 1992 analyzing the content of fifteen math, language arts, and history textbooks which were being used in Maryland, Virginia, and the District of Columbia, men and boys were shown to be represented two to three times as often as women and girls. In one well respected sixth grade history text published in 1992, the researchers found only seven pages out of 631 devoted to females; two of them were devoted to Samantha Smith, the fifth-grade Maine student who had visited the Soviet Union on a peace mission. Not a single adult American woman had been mentioned (Sadker and Sadker 1994, 72).

In addition to being left out of formal classroom material, issues which are of crucial importance to the lives of adolescent girls are often neglected, according to the AAUW report. These issues include such things as the politics of power, the health and functioning of girls' and women's bodies, explorations of their own feelings and emotions, and violence and abuse. One twelfth grade African American girl interviewed for the study stated succinctly: "In twelve years of school, I never studied anything about myself" (AAUW 1992, 61).

Gender Stereotyping in the Schools

One of the most important, and most damaging, lessons girls learn in school is to channel their energies in exclusively traditional and "feminine" ways. According to the results of a longitudinal study of 100 eight- to eighteen-year-old girls attending a private school in Ohio, girls at the school were taught by adults to be "nice" even when this meant disregarding their own feelings of anger, jealousy, boredom, etc. This "lesson" has the effect, for those girls who learn it, of dividing their outer (public) from their inner (private) selves. Girls in the study spoke of not being able to figure out who they really were, or what they really wanted (Brown and Gilligan 1992). Jennifer, a twelve-year-old, describing a conflict situation with a girl she did not like, illustrates this dividedness:

> I don't want to make someone upset 'cause that would get me into the depression age again and if I got them upset it would be a load on my mind and I'd hate myself and I'd try to get them to like me again . . . 'cause I liked being liked even though I don't like somebody (Brown and Gilligan 1992, 178).

Other studies have found that teachers influence girls to have lower expectations for themselves than boys have (Parsons, Kaczala, and Meece 1982), and that secondary teachers reward dominant, independent, and assertive behavior in boys and submissive, dependent, unassertive, and emotional behaviors in girls. In addition, girls are rewarded by teachers for their appearance much more often than boys are (Levy 1972).

In a study of vocational counseling for girls conducted by Wider Opportunities for Women, a national employment organization based in Washington D.C., 46 percent of female guidance counselors in three New Jersey communities believed that there "should be men's and women's jobs, and that girls ought to be prepared for the female jobs" (1993). Thus, the very institutions that should be encouraging girls to explore, achieve, and risk, are found to be efficient instruments of the androcentric value system. For as Mikel Brown notes: "The very behaviors adults praise in girls—compliance, selflessness, silence—are the same behaviors that are going to drop them out of the competition in the work force" (Brown 1993, 44).

CONCLUSION

I hope that readers will not have gotten the impression that traditional girls' roles and interests—in relationships and nurturing—are bad things. Quite the opposite is true, in fact. Girls' and women's lives in families, and in careers, will always be shaped by their relational/ connectional orientation to life. What is risky to girls is that the things they are taught to do well and to value are, as Brown says, the precise things that will keep them from achieving in a culture that values autonomy and competition.

Sadly, this is also true in the church. Theologian Rebecca Chopp describes how important "women's work" is for the church, and yet how it is often devalued: "Women's bonding, that which has often filled the pews, taught the children, baked the bread, done the dishes, and sewed the quilts, has not been the central order of the church" (1989, 75). The work women are taught to do well, by their families and schools, is often shoved to the "margins." The real power inheres in "men's work" even though, as Chopp points out, "women's work" (traditionally defined) often holds the church together, perpetuates its mission, and even constitutes the heart of the church's ministry.

What should be the church's response to this problem for both men and women? Churches should move in two directions: (1) The work and values which women traditionally hold need to be respected and given more status in the church; and (2) both women and men need to be made aware of gender stereotyping and to be trained to "do each other's work." Girls and women need to be given access to men's traditional work and to learn to be comfortable with it. Boys and men need to learn relational skills and to be comfortable exercising them. Girls who are discriminated against and made "invisible" in schools because their values and skills are not the same as boys', should find their churches to be places of encouragement and equality.

Jesus' life and ministry can be used as a model for this kind of respect for and advocacy of women. Jesus did not find women unimportant, outrageous, or bothersome. He valued women's work, and he let them know that he did, even in the face of those who would have ignored or despised them. As illustrated in this story from Mark, Jesus also understood and cared for young girls:

> Then came one of the rulers of the synagogue, Jairus by name; and seeing him, he fell at his feet, and besought him, saying, "My little daughter is at the point of death. Come and lay your hands on her so that she may be made well, and live." And he went with him. . . . While he was still speaking there came from the ruler's house some who said, "Your daughter is dead. Why trouble the Teacher any further?". . . And when [Jesus] had entered [Jairus' home] he said to them, "Why do you make a tumult and weep? The child is not dead but sleeping." Mark 5: 22–24, 35, 39

The report of Jesus' actions with Jairus' unnamed twelve-year-old daughter illustrates his ministry to her. According to Mark's account

Jesus first protected Jairus' daughter, limiting access to her to her close
family members and three disciples. Second, he (depending on inter-
pretation) either awakened her from a deep sleep or awakened her from
death itself with his authoritative, yet tender and respectful voice.
Third, upon her awakening, he challenged her to walk, and he called for
food to sustain and nurture her.

The task of pastoral care for girls is similar to the ministry Jesus had
with this twelve-year-old girl: to enable them to empower themselves
(when they are ready) to stand and walk. As caregivers, we can assist
girls in reclaiming the visibility that is often taken from them in their
schools; we can help them to hear their own voices, and to reflect on
the implications of their voices for their public worlds. These goals can
be achieved in many different ways—some of which take a large amount
of time and energy on the part of the pastoral or volunteer staff and
some of which evolve naturally out of a new way of valuing and listening to girls' experience.

First, girls should be given the opportunity to be in intentional relationships with women who are leaders in the church and in the outside
world. This has been accomplished in many churches by having an
older woman sponsor girls through, for example, the confirmation process or other "coming of age" time or ritual. One church initiated an
especially innovative year-long program which involved retreats, visits
at a woman's workplace or home, and collaboration on service projects.
The women and girls came to know and understand one another in
ways which they didn't expect. They worked and talked together; they
experienced setbacks and frustrations, and they experienced the tri-
umph of finished projects. They were accountable to one another and
to the church, and many reported becoming friends as well as partners
during the process.

Second, girls who are successful as athletes, musicians, scholars, en-
trepreneurs, animal-raisers, artists, etc., need to be given full recognition and encouragement in the church. Too often successful girls'
accomplishments are not noticed, because they are not the kinds of
achievements which normally make the "headlines" or even the gossip
columns. Several churches which I visited in the process of writing this
book had exciting programs in which girls' gifts and talents were actively cultivated. One church had a dance troupe; another allowed the
youth group to design a worship service in which the musicians, danc-
ers, artists, and actors were all given important roles and assignments.
Other churches made sure that youth who were thoughtful and good
speakers were given opportunities to read the scriptures and offer

prayers during worship. One church had an auditorium filled with musical instruments—electric guitars, amplifiers, microphones, etc.—for both boys' and girls' use after church and during youth group meetings. Another church published the accomplishments and activities of the graduating seniors, letting the seniors write their own articles about themselves.

It is often surprising to hear what girls will say when they talk about their accomplishments. Those things about which they are the proudest are often unrecognized by adults, who often have a more narrow range of focus. Where we may look at grade point averages, college acceptance letters, and won/loss records, the girls may be proudest of a poem written, an afterschool job, or a friendship restored.

Finally, girls should be taught to see themselves as "actors" in their own lives, not victims. It is true that girls "start from behind" in many ways; pastoral caregivers need to help them to understand this and to normalize the pain, anger, and frustration they may feel. It is also true that teaching girls that they are oppressed, apart from teaching them skills of resistance, is disempowering and unethical.

One of the church's major tasks in the care of adolescent girls is to nurture them, to help them find a place for their stories in the story of the church and specifically in the stories of women who have struggled with oppressive systems. Girls need to hear the stories of biblical women, the lives of the early Christian women, the courage of the martyrs, the passion of the mystics. They need to hear the stories of those persecuted by the church—the witches of the Middle Ages and New England Puritanism, the Jewish women under the German Church and Hitler. They need to hear stories of the heretics—Anne Hutchinson, Joan of Arc, Ann Lee, and the stories of social reformers—Dorothy Day and Jane Addams. They also need to be introduced to present day church reformers. As pastoral caregivers we are in a good position both to introduce girls to their heritage and to make a place for them and initiate them into their individual callings.

Through education in the church girls can learn to interpret the world, to develop strategies of resistance to being devalued, and to translate their thoughts and feelings into those which ultimately can be *heard* by the world. Peer support groups can be organized where girls take leadership roles and expand the process of defining themselves in relationship to others. These groups serve both to socialize them into a female culture, and to provide a testing ground for new thoughts, feelings, and plans. Girls can also be challenged to begin their work in the world and church—including work that does not only, or necessarily, provide emotional caregiving to others. In this work—which Marian Wright Edelman calls "the rent we pay for living"—girls begin to test themselves, and to "get up and walk" as Jairus' daughter did (Edelman 1992, 5–6).

The church in these days is in a unique position to protect and listen to adolescent girls, and to assist in the integration of their private and public voices. If the church carries out this ministry, then girls will speak with less hesitation and new power, and they will be heard.

2

GIRLS' PSYCHOLOGY

In chapter 1 we saw how a girl's experience begins in her family where, more often than not, she is trained to be a caretaker. Along with her mother and sisters she is charged with nurturing relationships and family harmony. Thus, she is prepared for a life in the private realm. When she enters school, this preparation is reinforced. Her contributions are not taken as seriously as the boys' in her classes. She is probably counseled to take traditional "female" subjects, and toward a traditional "female" occupation. By the end of her high school years she may be depressed and underachieving.

This chapter will deal with the major *internal* psychological developmental task which occupies girls during adolescence: the formation of an adult identity. During adolescence a girl's body takes the shape of a woman's; she begins to move out into the world as a young person in her own right. Her relationship with her family changes. Her intellect becomes more mature—able to do adult-type theorizing and hypothesizing. Her relationships with boys change (whether her sexual orientation is homosexual or heterosexual). And, the world seems full of new possibilities and dangers.

For boys the process of taking on an adult male identity, as it is described by developmental psychologists, is fairly straightforward. A boy, who has learned from his very early socialization to separate from his mother and others, takes this separation a step further in developing his own identity. He becomes his own man, with his own ideas, dreams, and plans. He will find ways to reconnect with others as he grows older, and is ready to test his new identity in relationships as a young adult.

For adolescent girls the process is not so easy; they have not experienced the relational break with their mothers and others in early childhood. For a girl to become a woman she must simultaneously (1) find her own separate identity—that which distinguishes her from her family and friends and (2) find ways to remain connected to those she loves.

Developmental psychologist Erik Erikson describes the ways in which both adolescent boys and girls work to find their own identities in his idea of the "identity crisis." For boys, Erikson's process describes the whole struggle; for most girls Erikson's theory describes half of what she must accomplish.[1] The second half of a girl's process of identity formation is described by Carol Gilligan; it is the process of coming to "truth" about the self and how the self negotiates relationships.

THE ADOLESCENT IDENTITY CRISIS

As is well known, Erik Erikson outlined eight stages in an individual's life: infancy, early childhood, play age, school age, adolescence, young adulthood, adulthood, and old age. Certain periods of life are marked by intense psychological tension which is usually initiated by bodily development. Erikson has termed these times of heightened tension "crisis" points.

The period of adolescence is a major turning point in any individual's life; it is a time of consolidations and new beginnings which drastically alter the youth's relationships and standing with the self, the family, and the surrounding culture. The crisis of adolescence is the problem of building a new adult identity. The adolescent's body is changing and developing, becoming adult in both appearance and function. Sexual maturity brings with it new energies along with new problems of appropriate expression and control; new physical and intellectual prowess also pose different challenges and expectations. Coming to a sense of individual identity is also a matter of relationships with the individual's wider circle of social acquaintances. Within the family and social spheres the adolescent must find a new way of *being*—not yet an adult in responsibilities and tasks, yet no longer a child.

Having an established identity means having a conscious sense of personhood and having feelings of appropriate belonging and fidelity to one's community and its institutions. A sense of inner identity—in relation to the self and society—is necessary both to complete the tasks of childhood and to begin to move forward to the new tasks of adulthood. It means becoming a person on one's own and establishing a place for one's self in the adult community.

There is a sense of painful self-consciousness in this period as adolescents become aware not only of themselves, but also that others are watching them and have expectations for them. Adolescents become most aware of their identities just before they actually gain them; the process is comparable to a "double-take" in the movies—youths see their identities and are somewhat surprised to make their own acquaintance. The new identity is surprising, yet it does not arise from nothing—it is based on and contains elements of all of the previous childhood stages.

Most societies recognize on some level that the pressure of identity formation should be met with reduced expectations of individuals experiencing this stage of life. The adolescents' communities are responsible to see that they are given the time, space, and encouragement to find their own rightful selves. Identity formation becomes a process of mutual recognition between an individual and a society—adolescents come to reject and accept parts of their previous childhood selves and to see how they are finally going to be related to their societies. Societies come to recognize and accept new members. Even as recognizing a new identity is often surprising for the adolescent, it is also often just as astonishing for his or her community. Often there may be initial resistance to the new identity on the part of the community, but in time those around the adolescent may feel honored to be asked for recognition.

Societies, thus, have a stake in making sure that individuals have a chance to develop and mature well. Often adolescents are given (or insist upon) what Erikson terms a "psychosocial moratorium" on adult responsibilities in order to accomplish this goal. This is a period of time between childhood and adulthood in which the individual can somewhat playfully test new and different roles—intellectual, emotional, occupational, and social. It is often a time for extended study, travel, military service, etc. Although the period is characterized by playfulness, it often results in deep commitments, almost in spite of the adolescent's intentions. It often ends in some kind of ceremonial confirmation of recognition of the coming of age of the adolescent on the part of society (Erikson 1959, 1968).

For girls this process of forming an identity often involves tricky negotiations. Not too many years ago, as Simone de Beauvoir wrote, a girl's options were so few that the question of her adult identity was settled almost as soon as she reached puberty:

> The young girl will be a wife, grandmother; she will keep house just as her mother did, she will give her children the same care she herself received when young—she is twelve years old and already her story is written in the heavens (de Beauvoir 1968, 278).

Today, it is much more probable that a girl will reach the age of adolescence and decide that she is not necessarily satisfied with traditional roles. Because identity formation is a two-way street, and because it cannot be completed until the society—her family, friends, school, and church— accepts the identity she presents to them, a girl may find herself stuck in a kind of limbo. The culture wants her to be relational and private. She is comfortable with relationality and yet wants experience in the public world.

Girls seem to have three choices at this point: (1) conscious or unconscious *compliance* with the intentions of the culture and abandoning of important parts of their identities, (2) *positive resistance* to the culture in modes which enhance the girls' newly emerging capabilities and sense of who she is, or (3) *negative resistance* to the culture by acting out destructively.

Negative Identities

Youth leaders and parents must be aware that there are times when girls will take on identities which seem to repudiate totally the church's and/or family's values. This is a more serious form of resistance, and it is often (but not always) self-destructive or in other ways negative. Erikson has termed these *negative identities*—that which the girl "has been warned *not* to become, which [she] can become only with a divided heart, but which [she] nevertheless finds [herself] compelled to become" (Erikson 1958, 102).

A girl's choice for a negative identity is an attempt to retain some control where she feels that all other choices will be destructive for her. When a girl chooses a negative identity, she is usually acting out her family's worst fears for her. If, for example, parents have persistently warned a girl about becoming a drug addict, she may begin to take drugs—if she feels there is no other hope for an identity which is not surrendering her own sense of who she is. If parents warn a girl about being an "unwed mother" but she feels (consciously or unconsciously) that there are no other viable identities for her, she may (unconsciously) seek to become pregnant. The same can hold true for many other kinds of "warnings" about whatever the family most fears for its members. These negative identities are often idiosyncratic for families and may not necessarily seem negative to outsiders. For one family it may be seen as very negative to "end up a waitress"; for others it may be negative to "end up a lawyer."

When a girl feels that all of the "positive" identities which are presented to her are in some ways impossible or unpalatable, the negative identity may seem to be the only choice available. This choice, however, is often made in the context of deep guilt and anger. In this way, parents' fears for their girls can be as powerful as their hopes are (see chapter 4).

A minister who cares for a girl who has taken on a negative identity must remember that this identity is often very painful and confusing for her as well as for the family members. Remember also that it was originally chosen (consciously or unconsciously) as a strategy of survival—when all other options seemed unrealistic and dangerous. Often these identities are transitory; unfortunately they are also often very self-destructive.

Carol Gilligan and Girls' Development

Carol Gilligan, a pioneer scholar in the work on female psychological and moral development, describes the journey she believes a girl makes as she begins to enter puberty and young womanhood, making her formal entrance into the adult world: "As the river of a girl's life flows into the sea of Western culture, she is in danger of drowning or disappearing. . . . She must enter—and by entering disrupt—a tradition in which 'human' has for the most part meant 'male' " (Gilligan, Lyons, and Hanmer 1990, 4).

Of central interest for Gilligan in her studies of young women's psychology was her finding that preadolescent girls seemed to have significantly fewer psychological problems than the older adolescents and women she had studied and written about in earlier research (Gilligan 1982). She found preadolescent girls to be remarkably free of conflict, self-doubt, and indirection; their voices were unburdened by indecision or hesitation. They were typically strong-willed, self-assured, and even "bossy."

Preadolescent girls seem ready to take on the world. They overcome obstacles; they are not conformists; they are problem-solvers. They are the type of individuals our culture values for inventiveness and courage. They are the type of people who don't let social structures get in their way, or even slow them down much. A recent news item about two particularly adventurous eleven-year-old girls provides a good illustration of the characteristics Gilligan describes:

> Two eleven-year-old girls determined to see a newborn niece secretly borrowed a grandfather's car, piled clothes on the front seat so they

could see over the steering wheel and drove more than ten hours. They
made it from West Virginia into Kentucky without a problem except for
getting lost in Lexington.

"Neither one of them had ever driven a car before," said . . . the
county juvenile case worker. "The parents were shocked. They didn't
think they had it in them to do it . . . [but] they did get to see the baby,"
he said (*The Dallas Morning News*, 11/2/91).

In contrast to these dauntless warrior preadolescent girls, however,
were the older adolescents and women in Gilligan's studies, who were
often unable to articulate their own thoughts or to speak their own
minds, much less plan deeds of derring-do! In her groundbreaking
book *In a Different Voice*, Gilligan described three typical themes in the
older adolescent girls' and women's developmental sequence: (1) survival, (2) goodness, and (3) truth. These themes (or loosely defined
"stages") have to do with relationships and connections; women
struggled with strategies for life and health in the context of complicated relationships and complex moral decisions.

The first theme in the women's struggle was *survival*—it involved
the terror of feelings of being alone, helpless, and abandoned. The
second theme, *goodness*, was a strategy for avoiding this terror, either by
becoming a "good" woman—willing to care for others and neglect
herself, or by becoming a culturally defined "selfish" woman—caring
for herself to the neglect of others. These two options were often seen
by the women to be mutually exclusive, and Gilligan reports that she
found women were often driven to desperate measures to fulfill the cultural and familial mandate of goodness. These measures often included
becoming and staying involved in harmful relationships, and/or becoming pregnant in order to feel connected to *someone*.

The third, and most positive, level of development according to Gilligan's studies, is a concern for *truth*—specifically truths about relationships. Gilligan discovered that there were some women in her studies
who were able to resist living at the second, or "goodness," level.
These women ultimately rejected "goodness" for several reasons. First,
it was psychologically untenable—they desired to live in relationship
with others without sacrificing themselves. Second, they found it impossible to live without pretence and deceit on the "goodness" level;
they observed themselves "plotting" ways to care for themselves in the
guise of caring for others. A concern to transcend the dichotomy of
caring for self or caring for others led these women to the truths that:
(1) relationships require the real presence of both the self and the other,
and (2) caring for others requires economic and social resources, such

as good employment and accessible health care, which are often not forthcoming for women in this culture.

For ethnic minority girls and women these struggles seemed to be even more pronounced. They must take on the task of forming a *racial* identity in addition to a workable identity as a woman. Janie Victoria Ward, an African American educator and social scientist, writes:

> In the face of glaring contradictions between the black experience as non-blacks believe it to be, and the black experience that the black adolescent knows it to be, the task becomes one in which the black child must unravel the faulty and dangerous attacks upon her identity, both individual and group (1990, 219).

The African American girl, according to Ward, must both resist—"I am *not* what you say I am," and affirm, "I *am* African American." If this process of positive identification with her African American community and traditions is not completed, the girl's identity formation as a whole is at risk. It is interesting to note that of all adolescent girls, African American girls consistently have the highest level of self-esteem when tested (AAUW 1992). Perhaps this is because many African American communities make very specific and important places for women as family and spiritual leaders.

The Power to Resist

Gilligan argues that the singular strength of the adolescent girl is her ability to observe life and relationships. This ability allows her to *resist* in some measure, the fate the culture would bestow on her. On the basis of Gilligan's interviews with adolescent girls she concluded that they have knowledge about adult "reality" and relationships that is often more accurate than the adults' own versions. Their perceptions are not often represented in social scientific literature, and, tragically, they are often disclaimed by the girls themselves. Gilligan compares their secret knowledge to a hidden cave: "I felt at times [when talking with the girls] that I was entering an underground world, that I was let in by girls to caverns of knowledge, which then suddenly were covered over, as if nothing was known and nothing was happening."

Because they know the world as a hostile place, unwilling to accept them and their insights, girls retreat "underground" to their own ultraprivate worlds. This retreat can be seen as a kind of resistance—a resistance which makes survival possible for them. Yet, tragically, this is not the kind of resistance which can produce positive change in the powerful public realm. Caregivers, both male and female, need to demonstrate extreme sensitivity toward this realm—both in respecting its boundaries and in supporting girls in other kinds of resistance.

CONCLUSION: THE CAREGIVER'S ROLE

As caregivers for adolescent girls we are called to be in unique relationship with them. The underground world which Gilligan describes, this site of secret knowledge, is the place where girls' true lives are often carried on away from the eyes of those apt to misunderstand or devalue. We may catch a glimpse of this place in overheard conversations, in the giggles, rolled eyes, sighs and other body language we observe, and in messages scribbled on blackboards and restrooms. Most of us, however, will not be invited into that world directly. Our exclusion is for many reasons, including our own socialization as men and women, and our positions of authority and responsibility over the girls. Girls probably expect that we will discount them and their experiences, or that we may even use their insights against them.

Against all our of inclinations as caregivers, and all of our best intentions to come to understand them, we need to respect the girls with whom we work, and to respect their right to have secrets. Remembering their socialization in families and schools (which aims to please us and to do what we expect of them) we must resist the temptation to ask them to "tell all" when they feel they need to protect themselves from our eyes and ears. Except in emergency situations (such as suspected physical abuse, drug and alcohol dependency, or eating disorders, which will be discussed in later chapters) we need to resist any impulses we may have to investigate their personal matters. We should not intentionally eavesdrop on conversations; we should not read their notes to each other; we should hold ourselves to the highest standards of integrity with regard to their lives and their worlds.

By the same token when a girl has concerns and wants to share them with us, we need to be careful that we respect her and the matter at hand—no matter how small it may at first seem to be to us. She may be "testing the waters" with us. She may wonder if we will take her seriously. She may be hoping that one of us will be a trustworthy and safe person for her—a refuge in the world she is coming to know.

But, while avoiding transgression into girls' private underground worlds, what positive roles might we, as pastoral caregivers, play in the development of adolescent girls' identities? Taking our cue from Erikson's work, we need to become a part of the accepting community—the group that notices and receives the newly emerging adult with gratitude and perhaps with surprise. We need to be those who notice a girl who is beginning to assert her adult self, to appreciate the struggle she is going through, and to encourage every positive and healthy development. This is a very difficult task, because it involves expanding our own views of what might be positive, healthy, and faithful. God speaks to each generation and each individual in new ways; we need to be open to hear the Spirit's voice as new women are being formed. Sometimes the developments may be personally painful for ministers and youth group leaders.

One pastor described a particularly difficult counseling session with a seventeen-year-old graduating senior in his church. She and he had had a very good relationship for her last three years of high school; she had been president of the youth group, and had earned several scholarships to good colleges in the area. Shortly before graduation, she came into his office for "advice" about college. After a few minutes of small talk, she reminded him that her ultimate career goal was to become a "child psychologist," because "I love children, and want to make their lives better." Thinking that she wanted to talk about psychology, he talked with her for a few minutes about psychology classes he had taken in college. When he noticed that she didn't appear very interested, he stopped talking and asked her if there was something else she wanted to discuss. At that invitation, she began to cry and announced, "I think God is calling me to the ministry." When he wondered aloud why she would be crying about that, she sobbed, "I have so much higher expectations of myself." This was a hard moment, but an important one for both the pastor and the young woman. The pastor relates that after taking several deep breaths, he was able to help her talk about her ambivalence, and ultimately to begin to assure her that God did not want anything for her that would be less than the best she could give. He also related that the shock of hearing this young woman's honest struggling with her own (seemingly negative) estimation of *his* profession, gave him a new way to understand the anger and pain (and even shame) of those who feel devalued.

It is probably more normal, however, for pastors to feel that the young women in their churches have set their sights too low. Many pastors talk about feeling helpless, in the face of traditional expectations, to encourage girls to see beyond the narrow horizons of their communities. Even in congregations where one might expect horizons to be wider, girls often speak of their goals exclusively in terms of "feminine" pursuits—involving caregiving and nurturing. These are, of course, not bad in themselves, but they are limiting for many girls.

In these situations it is important to provide models, to listen carefully, and to nurture any kinds of positive resistance that might be appropriate and helpful. Inviting women to preach and be lectors, taking the youth group on college tours, talking about women in the news, encouraging girls' athletics, making sure that the youth group does nongender specific activities and de-emphasizes gender stereotypes, helping girls to obtain afterschool work in nontraditional places, and doing everything possible to encourage girls to stay in school (including sexuality education) are some ways in which pastors and youth leaders can encourage girls to develop identities that are not overly tied to negative or low community expectations. For, as stated above, until communities and our culture at large become more girl-friendly, young women must learn to do the delicate balancing act necessary to live within their communities while also achieving what is necessary for their own health and salvation.

3

GIRLS' SPIRITUALITY

I'm feeling good today. After yesterday at church I feel at
peace with myself. It's like I'm renewed. I've been telling people
how I've found the Lord. They say I shouldn't play with God,
meaning I shouldn't go around talking about how touched I
am when I know I'm not. Well, even if this turns out to be a
phase, I know right now I'm really close to God.
      —Latoya Hunter, age twelve, *The Diary of Latoya Hunter*

In one sense, starting to understand adolescent girls by looking at their spiritualities is starting at the very deepest place in their secret underground worlds—the worlds we need to respect and not to transgress. As religious people, however, we believe that we cannot really begin to understand someone unless we learn about her spirituality—her "way of being in the world" (Procter-Smith 1990, 164). A girl's spirituality provides foundation for her life; it constitutes her rational and nonrational thinking about herself, and gives her a sense of who she is, how her life has meaning, how she relates to the cosmos, to others, and to God. Spiritual life is "life at the center" (Habito 1993, 30).

Obviously we will never come to know any girl totally, even a girl to whom we are very close; every girl remains mysterious no matter how much we know about her. Nevertheless, we must try to learn as much as we can about adolescent girls' spiritualities if we are to be in any sense caregivers for them. Part of my preparation for this book was listening to a good number of girls talk about their own feelings and beliefs, through a questionnaire and subsequent interviews of forty-four girls. (See Appendix.)

Although an attempt was made to talk to as wide a range of girls as possible from the standpoint of ethnic, geographic, age, economic and religious background, the girls who who eventually participated were informally recruited on the basis that they were willing to discuss their spirituality with me. Some shared what they considered to be very important experiences and beliefs; others were more reticent. A frequent, and disheartening, question from them to me was, "Why are you asking me this? Who would want to know what *I* think?"

As I noted in the Introduction, there is no one "adolescent girl"—and obviously there is no one spirituality which "fits" all adolescent girls. Indeed, as would be expected, the forty-four girls who participated revealed a wide range of both beliefs and experience. Some issues that were of great importance to eleven-year-olds were of passing interest to eighteen-year-olds and vice versa. Some issues that were pressing for the urban African American girls were not even raised by most of the Anglo girls. The girls from rural Texas experienced different kinds of problems from those of the girls from suburban Boston. And, the girls from families of wealth had some very different concerns from those whose families had fewer means.

Several *themes*, however, seemed to emerge naturally that appeared to have resonance across most of the geographic, economic, racial and age differences. This chapter will examine the most important of these themes: the girls' relationship to and image of God.

Each of the girls who participated in this project struggled in her own way with the limitations which are a part of her birthright in this culture. The girls wondered about God's will and career choices, about how to maintain relationships in the midst of conflict, about how to express their own faiths in the face of church restrictions or prohibitions, and about moral and ethical issues of sexuality and reproduction. Because of the cultural aspects of belief in and relationship to God, I have looked for two other *overarching* themes in the girls' responses: (1) *compliance* and (2) *resistance*. Compliance is signified by evidence that girls have internalized cultural limitations and devaluation of women. Resistance is signified by girls' unwillingness to participate in cultural oppression of themselves and other girls and women.

Finally, this chapter will offer strategies for work with adolescent girls that will encourage development of positive and empowering images of God and personal spiritualities. It will especially focus on helping girls to *resist* culturally presented images of God which may be harmful, and on helping them to transform unconscious *compliance* with limiting cultural values into conscious choices against these values. Recognizing and working with these two themes in the area of spirituality becomes the foundation for the entire enterprise of pastoral care with adolescent girls.

BELIEF IN AND RELATIONSHIP WITH GOD

In addition to being a response to God's revelation to us as individuals, belief in God is also a response to social and psychological processes. No girl comes to a belief in God by herself. She is aided and supplied information about God from many sources, including her church, family, and her culture. In most cases a child is originally introduced to God in her family by her parents. Then her biological family introduces the child to church, where she learns special stories, rules, and rituals relating to God, and she becomes a part of a larger family of faith. Finally when a child is old enough she begins to become aware of cultural manifestations of belief in God in art, architecture, and social events which may or may not take place in a church or other house of worship (e.g., funerals, weddings, swearing-in in court, civil ceremonies, etc.).

Anna Maria Rizzuto has shown how all of these social elements of faith combine with a child's psychological experience and makeup to form a "composite" image of God which each individual carries with him or her. This image is relatively stable in most people, but it is continually refined on the basis of our learning, experiences, and maturity. Just as, according to Rizzuto, "no child arrives at the 'house of God' without [her] pet God under [her] arm," (Rizzuto 1979, 8), no adolescent girl arrives in our office or youth group without a God image that is unique to her.

The girls' responses to questions about God were simple yet incredibly sophisticated. Their images of God were extremely complex, nuanced, and often paradoxical. They were, of course, in many ways reflective of their cultural heritages—including both positive and negative influences. They were also often strikingly original and thought-provoking. Some are definitely nontraditional; most evidenced creative struggle between orthodoxy, as they understood it, and unorthodox personal faith. In general their images fell into three different but overlapping categories: God as a benevolent man, the God who transcends ethnicity, and the God who overcomes dualities.

God as a Benevolent Man

The most striking and obvious similarity in the girls' responses to the part of the questionnaire dealing with their images of God was God's resemblance to male figures with whom they were acquainted. Most drew or wrote about God as a man or man-like creature. These pictures and descriptions ranged from full-bodied pictures of male Episcopal priests in albs with crosses, to disembodied faces with moustaches and beards. One older girl, who admitted that she did not have much time for spirituality ("the time for religion is later—I'll try it at college") nevertheless drew a whimsical, big-eared, smiling head with a goatee: "I don't believe in God, but this is my picture!"

For all those who pictured God as a male, he was a benevolent figure. One eleven-year-old drew God as a protector/angel: "I made him an angel because he is not a person but he is protective. He can't be seen so he could be a gardean [guardian] angel." Another sees God as a supernatural helper: "I believe God is like a ghost-angel. He comes around and helps people at bad times. He is like a ghost-angel because he can not be seen, he can only hear." One older girl said although she felt "silly" saying it, her idea of God was like her best friend from nursery school's father who had been very kind to her.

The God Who Transcends Ethnicity

The color of God's skin was especially important to the African American and Hispanic girls who participated. For these girls God (sometimes identified as Jesus) was either no color, all colors, or dark-skinned.

One fourteen-year-old who identified herself as African American drew a man's face for God with dark skin, black hair, beard, and moustache. She was not completely happy with this picture, nevertheless it was the only one she could produce: "This is all I could think of since it is the first thing that came to me. When I think of God there isn't a clear picture, I can just feel his presence somewhere." Another sixteen-year-old African American wrote: "I don't think that God has a certain color or shape. But I do know that he is a supreme being and is everywhere." An eleven-year-old who identified herself as "Afro-American" drew a picture of a dark-skinned man with black hair in a bright green robe and wrote: "God is a darker color like [an] Indian's because he is from the east (according to the Bible)."

Although these girls did not seem to resist the cultural message that God is male, they were indeed in touch with the fact that the traditional image of a white God was not true. They knew that *if* God had a skin color, somehow their own skin color was represented in God. Perhaps the saddest description of God in terms of ethnicity and gender, however, came from an eighteen-year-old who identified herself as Mexican American:

> My picture of god is the one I've been shown since I was little. It's the traditional white, light brown hair, blue-eyed God people hang pictures

of in their home. I wouldn't know how else to describe him. Perhaps he's a little more aged if people age in another life.

For this girl, God's image did not reflect her race, her gender, or her age. God was someone different than she was—an older white man whose picture is a decoration in her home. In her response she made no attempt to see God's image reflected in herself, or to see herself reflected there in the picture on the wall. It is perhaps noteworthy that along with this rather distant and weak image of God she had an unusually weak (compared to the other girls) image of herself and her own ability to accomplish much in the world. In response to a later question about her hopes for the future she replied: "I just want to make a small difference, hopefully for the better, before I die."

A God Who Overcomes Dualities

For most of the girls, God cannot be described as a simple being; God is a complex intermingling of what seem to be polar opposites. Many of the girls were able to overcome the dualism inherent in the opposite images in fascinating and sophisticated ways: God is male and female; personal and impersonal; immanent (connected to nature by creation), and transcendent (sustaining the world from far above). And for those who reflected on the color of God's skin, most agreed that God either had no color or all colors.

An eleven-year-old who drew God as a bright yellow circle with a red and full-lipped, smiling mouth and outstretched arms wrote: "I think God is a bright light. The light is humungus and it can turn into anything it wants to be. I think it's a man. He can turn into a person, animal, or anything he created." The tension in this image is obvious and complex. God is an impersonal force—a light—yet also a man. In addition, God is able to turn into an animal or any other created thing.

She continues: "The light has hands coming out of it because they symbolize him reaching out to others. He also always has a smile on his face. The smile stands for happiness; he wants the best for the world." This simple description represents a powerful combination of traditional male and female aspects. The creator is man, yet "he" also has an interesting ability to take other forms—"any other created thing." The red-lipped smiling God also embodies the culturally feminine virtue of nurturing creation.

This girl seems to have found a way to incorporate both female and male images of God into an impersonal image of light—that "reaches out to others" and "wants the best for the world." On a later question she shows the effects of this image of God on her own self-image. She writes: "I feel God expects me to be myself because that's the way he made me." A creator God who somehow reflects her image in "his" nature, allows her to "be herself" as she was created by "him."

Another girl, a twelve-year-old who drew a rather androgynous face for her image of God wrote: "I believe that God is half woman and half man. I think that He/She is all human and a slight bit animal. He/She is a perfect example for an excellent citizenship award! He/She makes mistakes just like humans!"

This is another very complex image of God. Here again, we see an image that focuses on inclusion; "He/She" is identified with woman, man, and animal. God is identified with what is culturally accepted as the higher forms of creation. Yet God also, in some way, transcends these forms, by being the perfect citizen—a high value in her school culture. In all this, however, God never loses touch with humanity; even in God's perfection "He/She" makes mistakes "like humans."

Other girls described the same kinds of complexity. One drew an interesting picture of God with both male and female characteristics: a person with a moustache and curly long hair who appeared to be wearing a dress with a collar and buttons down the front. Her statement: "I think God looks like everybody and is everybody. He is every race, shape, and size." Another twelve-year-old wrote: "I don't think of God as having any physical characteristics. Just as a supreme being that is everywhere."

One particularly interesting (and unorthodox) eighteen-year-old drew God as the earth with the sun shining on it, and symbols of Gaia and Apollo surrounding it. She described God as "Gaia and Apollo/the Mother and Father." Gaia represents "earth, air, fire, and water" and Apollo represents "the sun, strength, warmth, and transcendence." Yet this representation is not complete for her; she states she is not really ready to make a commitment to one belief system or god: "At this point, I am not siding with any one organized religion. . . . I think my own personal religion, once built up, will be heavily into nature and the earth. My higher power would be the sun."

In response to a question about what she finds problematic about God she wrote: "I believe that every god ever worshipped exists, some have just fallen silent due to lack of followers. . . . I have trouble isolating the ones I choose to worship. Isis and Athena are some of my favorites." She also is aware of the developing nature of her religious belief: "As new answers (and new questions) arc found, these beliefs grow and change, and a response today may be totally different than the answer to the same question tomorrow."

This girl has chosen historic symbols of faith—male and female gods who embody transcendence (the sun) and immanence (the earth elements), yet she realizes that this is not yet mature faith for her. Her beliefs "grow and change." Many gods are real for her; her dilemma is to make a choice among them. Of her current choices the sun (male/Apollo) is her "higher power," but Isis and Athena (both female/both represent the moon) are her "favorites."

The religious experience that was most meaningful to her was "seeing aurora borealis" shining "bright red" when she was in ninth grade. "At the time it was just really neat but lately it's had an impact on my thinking about spiritual energy. It's like proof that Gaia (the earth) *does* have a living energy. It's my 'burning bush.' " Although this girl uses different historical images to describe her God, her quest is similar to those of the other girls: How can I find a God to believe in? How do I choose between representations? She seems to recognize a need to find a male image along with female images, and also to incorporate images of the power of her world, which she is coming to love and respect, with the power of the sun, which she sees as transcendent. Interestingly, she uses the Judeo-Christian image of the "burning bush" to describe the way in which the power of her religion became real to her.

IMPLICATIONS FOR PASTORAL CARE

These girls' responses regarding their personal images of God must make us as pastoral caregivers reflect carefully on several aspects of our work. The first has to do with male and female images of God. The second has to do with the complexity of the images which the girls described.

God as Exclusively Male

First, the implications for these girls, especially those of the first group, who believe in a God who is essentially male (even if they understand that the language is metaphorical) should not be underestimated. Theologians such as Rosemary Radford Reuther, Sallie McFague, Letty Russell, Rebecca Chopp, Elizabeth Johnson, and Carroll Saussy show us that the language we use to speak about God has profound implications for how we live together and what we believe about our entire lives:

> . . . the symbol of God functions as the primary symbol of the whole religious system, the ultimate point of reference for understanding experience, life, and the world. Hence the way in which a faith community shapes language about God implicitly represents what it takes to be the highest good, the profoundest truth, the most appealing beauty (Johnson 1992, 4).

For girls to see God exclusively as a man, or male figure, (even the most benevolent of males) is for them to be in compliance with one of the ways in which the Judeo-Christian tradition has most effectively exerted oppressive authority over women. For if "God is male, or at least more like a man than a woman, or at least more fittingly addressed as male than female . . . [then] women's human dignity as equally created in the image of God [is undermined]" (Johnson 1992, 5). If a girl's image of God is exclusively male, then her image of herself is probably disturbed.

W. E. B. DuBois in his powerful book, *The Souls of Black Folk*, describes a similar dynamic at work in the lives of African Americans in the early twentieth century. He perceived that the standard for "human culture" at the time was exclusively based on "white" culture. For African Americans, he wrote, there was the "problem" of being anomalous in the larger culture—not white but still human. This problem, as he termed it, did not allow a true self-consciousness to develop in black individuals or in the black community. What developed was a "double-consciousness" or "sense of always looking at one's self through the eyes of others, of measuring one's soul by the tape of a world that looks on in amused contempt and pity" (DuBois 1961 [1903], 16–17).

Something akin to this "double-consciousness" must also develop in girls and women who are, as they are assured in Genesis, made in the image of God, yet not represented in the available cultural images of God. How can a girl be made in the image of God if God is a man—even a benevolent man? If, with Barth, we assert that we know what it is to be human, because we know God who became human for our sakes, what does it mean that girls can see so little of themselves in the God represented to them by the authorities (parents, ministers, teachers) in their lives?

As pastoral caregivers we must be very sensitive to the images of God we employ in the pulpit, in the church school, in youth fellowship, and in the counseling office. We must also be sensitive to the images which

are being brought to us. Each girl will have her own unique way of putting together her experience with the teachings of her church and
family. As we work with girls on issues such as family problems, eating
disorders, drug and alcohol abuse, and sexual problems, we need to remember that a girl who has never seen herself reflected in any image of
God presented by the culture, family, or church will be starting from a
position of relative weakness. Carroll Saussy (1991) has suggested that
women may even need to be provided a "transitional space" in which
to experience God in exclusively female terms (as Goddess/Earth
Mother/Life Giver) to "claim the source of female beauty and power in
Deity," before they are able to experience God as inclusive of both
feminine and masculine.

In terms of compliance and resistance, a caregiver should help girls
look at the ways in which they unconsciously accept male images of
God. Help girls to look at their own image of God in terms of how it
reflects a belief in the gender of God: Do they always call God "father"
or "he"? Do they think of God with a beard? Do they think of God as
a "king"? Help them to wonder what other images might look like by
discussing Genesis 1—if we are (male and female) made in God's image
then what must God be like? Discuss Luke 15:4-10 where God is portrayed as a woman looking for a coin and as a man looking for a lost
sheep. And, especially, introduce them to the ways in which the Holy
Spirit is portrayed as female such as Genesis 1:2 where the Spirit moves
(or hovers) over creation (like a mother bird), and John 3:4-6 where
God's spirit is compared to a mother giving birth. The figure of
Wisdom/Sophia found in Job and Proverbs, and alluded to in the New
Testament, is the most fully developed picture of God in female form.[1]

Girls should be aware that their own traditions support images of
God that are both female and male. God's image includes them, and
therefore they can say, as did the twelve-year-old above, "God wants
me to be just who I am." Being a girl is fine in God's eyes.

The Complexity of God

Johnson believes that the kind of dualistic thinking with which the girls
wrestled (male/female; personal/impersonal, etc.) is at the heart of
women's struggle to find meaning in the Christian faith. Women are
trained in our culture to be relational and nurturing, yet most images of
God presented to women are insufficient to support relationship with
God. Along with female/male dualism, one of the most troubling du-
alisms for women which was clearly represented in the girls' responses is

that of immanence and transcendence. Neither the God image of the theists which is wholly transcendent, nor the God image of the pantheists which is wholly immanent can be satisfactory for women or girls, because neither is relational.

Johnson suggests a solution which is reflected in many of the girls' images of God, a *panentheistic* image of God. Panentheism is described as: "The belief that the Being of God includes and penetrates the whole universe, so that every part of it exists in [God], but . . . that this Being is more than, and is not exhausted by, the universe."[2] This panentheistic image allows a relationship between God and God's creation: "God in the world and the world in God while each remains radically distinct" (Johnson 1992, 230–231).

These problems may seem abstract, but as the girls show, they are the root of very real issues. How can I know God? How can God know me and the world? As one 12 year old theologian wrote: "I think God is the World because he created it. And he watches over us every day." God both *is* the world and *watches over* it. In fact God watches over "us"—the people of the world including her—at all times. God, as both transcendent and immanent, can at once be a part of the world and take care of it, can be in relationship with it while remaining distinct from it.

Some of us may believe in a God who does not change. If we are growing spiritually, however, our *images* of God must change all the time, in response to our own learning and experiences of life. As C. S. Lewis wrote after the death of his wife: "My idea of God is not a divine idea. It has to be shattered time after time. He shatters it himself. He is the great iconoclast. Could we not almost say that this shattering is one of the marks of his presence?" (Lewis 1966, 52).

We must also continually be aware that to shatter (or even to change slightly) a person's image of God is often to throw that person into a state of anxiety. As stated earlier, our spiritualities are at the center of who we are—they are the foundations of our world and our sense of relatedness to our environment and to other people. Images of God, as Rizzuto has shown, reside close to the center of our spiritualities. As caregivers we need to pay close attention to the images of God presented to us in counseling situations with girls. Does God feel too close—threatening to overpower or absorb? Is God too far off—powerful but distant? Images that fall too close to being either wholly transcendent or wholly immanent can be harmful. If God is too close, then personal identity is threatened. If God is too far away, then feelings of security and hope are endangered.

One of the most important tasks we share is helping others redefine and reimagine God (a process every person undertakes many times during his or her life as faith grows and matures). We should never attempt to force girls to abandon images of God which they feel are useful to them, even if we believe they are harmful. If possible, however, we should seek opportunities to help girls, in particular, become conscious of the ways in which their culturally inherited views of God may be destructive for them. And more positively, we are in positions where it may be possible to help them find images of God which are both truthful (in terms of our various traditions) and beneficial for their spiritual journeys. With a God who is for them, who can be against them?

4

GIRLS IN FAMILIES

*I have always been a very independent person, but my parents
and I have a very close relationship. . . . I couldn't live without
them, just knowing they are there.*

Sallie, age seventeen

Families at the end of the twentieth century look very different from
the ideal many people hold in their minds. Seminary classes on families
frequently begin by exploring the myth of the middle class family. This
myth, lamentably, is often connected to images presented in situation
comedies of years ago. Programs such as *Leave It to Beaver, Donna
Reed,* and *Father Knows Best* have left indelible impressions on the
American psyche. The families represented by them were all Caucasian.
In these families parents were heterosexual and married to each other;
mothers stayed at home and fathers left home to go to work; there were
usually two or more children; there was plenty to eat, and separate bed-
rooms for all the children; there was no violence and no drug or alcohol
abuse; and, of course, all problems were solvable in a half-hour or less.

Sociologists, family therapists, and ministers who have gotten to
know the families in their churches know that families today look much
different from these old television models. One important difference
for girls and women is that today both parents work outside of the
home in almost two-thirds of two-parent families (Hayghe 1990,
14–19). Families are also not permanent: It is currently estimated that
half of all marriages will end in divorce and that approximately 60% of
these dissolutions will involve children. It has been estimated that 38%
of Anglo children and 75% of African American children born to married parents in the United States will experience their parents' divorce
(Bumpass 1984, 71–82). It is predicted that 35% of children born

during the 1980s will live with a stepparent before they are 18 years old (Glick 1991).

For many years middle class Anglo families were taken as the standard of "normal," and other families were labeled as dysfunctional or problematic. Today family therapists are beginning to explore the differences between families of various cultures and ethnic backgrounds (Boyd-Franklin 1989; McGoldrick, Pearce, and Giordano 1982). Researchers are also just beginning to explore the dynamics of lesbian and gay families, which have been invisible in our culture until very recently (Laird 1993).

As was described in the first chapter, the family—with all its problems and diversity—is the place where girls first learn what it means to be a female in this culture. In most families (even most of those which think of themselves as not adhering to gender stereotypes) girls learn from both parents that although women may "minor" in outside work and careers, most usually "major" in relationships and caretaking. They also learn that men may "minor" in family relationships, but they usually "major" in more public and maintenance-oriented tasks.

It is also in the family that most girls learn about their faith and what it means to be a religious person. Two questions from the spirituality questionnaire especially illustrated the importance of family for adolescent girls. In the first of these, girls were asked to name the two most important values in their lives and the people in their lives who supported the girls in these values. The overwhelming majority of the girls who answered both parts of the question named their parents or their families as the ones who supported them. In the second of the questions girls were asked to name the person they most admired; two-thirds of the girls indicated that they most admired a family member—usually their mothers or their fathers.

This chapter explores the relationships girls have with their families—individual members and the family as a whole. First the highly charged and highly important relationship between mother and daughter—"the great unwritten story" (Rich 1986, 225)—is described. Next, the father-daughter relationship, which is undergoing great stress as the girl becomes more adult, is focused on. Third, the family as a system and the girl's part in it is explored. Finally, strategies will be recommended for dealing with two of the most common problems for families with adolescent girls: (1) communication problems and (2) rigid family roles.

GIRLS AND THEIR MOTHERS

As was described in the second chapter, the dual psychological tasks of adolescent girls are: (1) to become their own people—developing personal styles, firming up their individual identities, choosing a career path, and establishing personal values, and (2) to negotiate ways to remain in relationship with important other people (especially family and significant intimate others). Studies have shown over and over again that one of the most important relationships for the adolescent girl is with her mother. This relationship is so important to most girls that they may be reluctant even to speak about it with counselors; many are not fully ready to explore their relationships with their mothers until they reach adulthood. As Adrienne Rich writes:

> . . . Probably there is nothing in human nature more resonant with charges than the flow of energy between two biologically alike bodies, one of which has lain in amniotic bliss inside the other, one of which has labored to give birth to the other. The materials are here for the deepest mutuality and the most painful estrangement (1986, 225–226).

For most girls, their mothers are the persons with whom they have maintained the most powerful relationship since earliest childhood. In order for a girl to come to an adult identity she and her mother must go through an often painful series of negotiations. Both mothers and daughters must come to see each other in new ways. For many girls their mothers become models of what it means to be selves who are also in relationship with others (Kaplan, Gleason, and Klein 1991, 127).

Mothers, who often identify deeply with daughters, may unconsciously plan to live out their own unfulfilled dreams through them. They will perhaps go through periods of mourning for their own dreams as they learn to give up those aspects of their daughters which the daughters are trying to repudiate. Most mothers also recognize what they consider to be their own worst mistakes during adolescence and deeply desire to steer their daughters away from those. In healthy relationships, however, mothers must maintain relationships with the women their daughters are struggling to become—honoring their successes and respecting their mistakes.

Daughters, for their parts, must have the confidence that they can grow and change without being rejected by their mothers. They need to be able to give up childish ideas about their mothers—especially that mothers are able to provide perfect care and protection.

There are many ways in which the mother-daughter struggle becomes evident. One very common one is through a daughter's choosing of activities for herself which do not fit her mother's image of her. A mother who has her heart set on a daughter being a member of the cheerleading squad, or pep team may struggle deeply with a daughter who joins the girl's basketball team, or who chooses not to participate in extracurricular activities at all. A mother who hopes her daughter will be a top scholar may agonize over the daughter's choices to invest most of her energy outside of school.

Girls who are just beginning to negotiate their own ways in the world may often choose *against* their mothers' wishes as a form of resistance. This resistance, as we know, can take positive or negative forms. A positive form of resistance would be one in which the daughter was asserting a part of herself that she felt was essential and that she felt the mother was misunderstanding or rejecting.

A typical example of this kind of positive resistance would occur in a girl's choice of clothing and hairstyles. A girl who has previously been content with her mother's choice of plaid skirts and sweaters may "suddenly" decide that she only wants to wear flannel shirts and jeans. She may also decide to cut long hair; perm straight hair; straighten permed hair; or dye streaks of her hair green and blue. She may decide to pierce her ears once or twice (or more); she may get a tatoo—whatever she knows will displease or shock her mother the most.

Another frequently encountered example of positive resistance has to do with a girl's participation in religious events with the family. This resistance usually entails a girl's unwillingness to attend church functions, or her protestations about participating to her mother's satisfaction, as illustrated below:

> Gerry, the mother of an eighth-grade girl, called the youth minister at their church with a question: "What in the world do you think is happening to Robyn? She's changing right in front of my eyes. She quit the junior high band, she listens to weird and loud music all night in her room, and she refuses to wear dresses anymore to church. Worst of all she doesn't want to attend Sunday school. Can you please talk some sense into her and tell her that she needs to go to Sunday school?"

In this instance there is a clear mother-daughter identity struggle going on. The youth leader is being asked to enter the fray over the issue of Sunday school—one of many issues being presented. Entering into family disputes on this level is seldom a good idea and is never very successful in any case. Robyn's youth leader could be of invaluable assistance to Gerry and Robyn at this time by attending to the struggle *beneath* the request.

Gerry is afraid; she seems to be losing touch with her daughter. She is also, by the sound of it, engaged in a test of power with Robyn—"You *will* wear a dress to church! You *will* go to Sunday school." One can almost hear the "because I said so" tagged on—the one Gerry had sworn that she'd never use on her *own* children.

The youth leader who could hear all these issues will engage Gerry on the deeper level of mother-daughter struggle, rather than picking up on the issue of whether or not Robyn needs to go to Sunday school. The leader's job is to *normalize* some of this struggle for both Gerry and Robyn. Gerry can be helped to understand the process that Robyn is going through. She can, we hope, be helped to see that, although the individual issues about dresses, and music, and Sunday School may *feel* as if they are crucial (especially if Robyn has never really asserted herself before), none of them are matters of life and death, or even of extreme importance in the larger picture of what is taking place.

This youth leader could also perform another invaluable service for Gerry and Robyn by staying in close touch with the culture and dynamics of the girls and the youth group, and being able to be a "reality test" for them. If the leader knows the current likes, dislikes, styles, etc., of the group and also knows the current negative trends, he or she can either assuage the mother's fears about particular behaviors ("I know that music is distressing, but the lyrics on that album are actually pretty harmless, and a lot of kids are listening to it.") or warn her about behaviors that *do* seem dangerous ("I'm really worried about Robyn's choice of friends this year").

Robyn can be helped to channel in positive ways her resistance to her mother's idea of who she is. As parents, girls, and youth leaders know, there are many ways of making identity statements. Some of them are harmless (e.g., playing loud music and refusing to wear dresses to church); some of them are self-destructive (e.g., refusing to do schoolwork, taking drugs, having unhealthy sexual relationships). It is especially important at times when a particular girl or group of girls is undergoing changes, that youth leaders *listen* to them—to hear the particular ways they are struggling to grow and to affirm the positive aspects of that growth. It is also important that leaders not assume they know, before listening, what positive or negative resistance will look like for the girls they counsel.

For mothers and daughters who are not aware of the real issues with which they are dealing—namely the girls' testing and retesting of their identities—every issue can seem enormous. It is in this struggle, however, that girls can begin to learn an important lesson about what it means to be a self who is also in relationship. If a girl and her mother can come to understanding about how to be separate individuals yet remain in connection with each other, the girl will have a strong foundation on which to build other adult relationships. In Gilligan's terms she will have learned the *truth* that good relationships entail caring for the other and the self.

When to Refer to a Family Counselor

If a mother-daughter struggle is so intense or painful that it seems to be having enduring negative consequences for one or both of their lives, or it seems that they are at an emotional impasse, then the pastor should consider referring the family to a family counselor who specializes in women's issues and (preferably) is experienced in working with adolescent girls. Also, a pastor should refer if he or she knows about or suspects physical, sexual, or emotional abuse in the family. (See chapter 5.)

GIRLS AND THEIR FATHERS

As described above, the most important relational issue between mothers and their adolescent daughters is staying in relationship with each other while acknowledging the differences between them. For girls and their fathers identity issues take on a different tone. Girls' relationships with their fathers often take more playful forms than those with their mothers. Where mothers help them explore feelings, fathers help them play and be adventurous (Stiver 1991, 113–114). Because girls are usually not as emotionally connected with fathers as they are with mothers—fathers are the "outsiders" in the early childhood drama of connection and separation—a girl's new identity may be less personally threatening to a father. Fathers are more likely than mothers to encourage girls to be ambitious and to achieve in the public arena. Although gender roles are slowly changing, men's traditional "natural" realm is the public; men have been expected to introduce girls to what it means to have competence and mastery outside of the home.

For this reason a father's expectations of his daughter hold extreme importance for her. In the best cases, a father's support for his daughter becomes the validation she needs to confirm her own independent identity. A father who promotes his daughter's drive for achievement is telling her that a powerful part of her emerging identity is valued by those she loves. It is often difficult, however, in this androcentric culture, for fathers to figure out what it is, exactly, they expect from (or for) their daughters. As family therapist Betty Carter has pointed out, many men are filled with ambivalence about their hopes for their daughters:

> In middle-class families, father wants daughter to "succeed," but still sees marriage as the main goal for her. . . . He may spend a fortune on her education, but still not expect personal achievement of her. . . . He prides himself on his strength and competence, but then rewards compliance and dependency in his relationship with her (Carter 1988, 90).

One of the most frequent complaints that girls have about their fathers is that they do not feel respected by them. During adolescence girls are extremely sensitive to their fathers' feelings about them, and may assume they know their fathers' feelings when they do not. When (or if) a father seems not to be adjusting to his daughter's new and more mature identity, she probably feels this state is a rejection. Just as with her mother, a girl wants to feel valued by her father for being herself—the self that she is becoming. It is not enough for her that her father loves and respects her because "he has to—I'm his daughter!" Rather, she needs to feel that he *knows* her as a person, and loves and respects her for the young woman she is becoming.

A father, whether he realizes (or desires) it, represents the adult male world to his daughter. From her father a girl learns what it means to be in relationship with a man. In this culture, however, men often play out their ambivalence toward their daughters by teaching them negative lessons about what it means to be a woman. Fathers seem to enforce sex-role stereotyped behavior and conformity more than mothers. Studies have shown that girls' preference for traditionally "feminine" behaviors—being nice even when angry, being compliant, needing others to like them, and being overly concerned with appearance— relates more strongly to the encouragement of their fathers than to the "femininity" of their mothers (Kaschak 1992, 121, 93).

Another way in which girls learn what it means to be a woman is by watching their mothers and fathers interact. Sadly, while many adult men in therapy express the desire to emulate their fathers, many adult women in therapy express the desire to be the opposite of their mothers. Often women state this feeling in terms of feeling betrayed by mothers who were devalued in their families by their fathers—"Why didn't my mother fight harder to keep her dignity?" This dynamic has been found to be one (if not *the*) major cause of anger between adult daughters and their mothers (Lewis and Herman 1986, 150).

The implications of this situation are vast for both men and women. If a daughter sees her mother being devalued by her father, she experiences both a devaluation of herself and a realization that her own future holds little promise for reward or power. If a father wants to teach a girl to respect herself as a woman, it is incumbent on him to work with his wife on developing a mutually respectful relationship.

Compounding the problem of ambivalence about daughters' goals, fathers in many families find (or place) themselves on the "outside" during their daughters' adolescence. Fathers are often less involved with their daughters during their teenage years than they have been up to that point. Studies show that while fathers tend to be extremely attached and involved with their small daughters, closeness diminishes as girls reach puberty and adolescence. Girls talk to their fathers less, tell them less about their lives, spend less time with them, and in return receive less support and encouragement from them (Apter 1990, 74–75).

Part of the reason for the growing distance between fathers and adolescent daughters is the daughter's physical development into a woman. Where mothers may feel conflicted about their daughters' new adolescent sexuality—feeling a need to protect them while at the same time feeling proud and perhaps envious—fathers often feel confused. They often become awkward about relating with their daughters, unsure of how to handle closeness with a girl who is becoming more and more woman-like in appearance. Because men are not as adept at complex relationships as women are trained to be, fathers often withdraw, perhaps even becoming angry in order to maintain the distance they feel is necessary from their daughters.

Fathers often need encouragement to overcome their inhibitions in relating to their daughters emotionally. Men may feel the only way to remain close to their daughters is to sexualize the relationship. Most men reject this sexualizing, but truly do not know what the alternatives can be. A pastoral caregiver (whether male or female) can teach about and model appropriate relationships with girls. (See chapter 5.)

When to Refer to a Family Counselor

When a father-daughter relationship seems very remote or very conflicted, especially when there has not been a history of closeness, a pastor may consider referring to a family counselor. Also, as with mother-daughter problems, if a pastor knows about or suspects physical, sexual or emotional abuse he or she should refer. (See Chapter 5.)

THE FAMILY AS A SYSTEM

To this point we have looked at a girl's relationships with both her mother and her father as important factors in the way in which she forms her identity as a woman and as an adult. But, of course, the situation is much more complex than this. The form of relationship that a girl's mother has with her father also has serious implications for her feelings about herself. In addition, a girl also has a relationship to her family as a whole, and all of the relationships this involves. She probably has relationships with other family members—siblings, grandparents, aunts and uncles, and perhaps other extended family members. Caregivers also need to look at a girl's family as an entity in itself, a unit which is made up of multiple relationships—a family system.

A family systems approach is based on the observation that a family is a complex organization with *characteristics* different from the characteristics of any of the individual members and a kind of *power* different from and greater than the combined power of all of the individual members. Each single family member operates both as an individual and as part of the larger system.

A good illustration of this individual/system interaction is a mobile, with individual parts all connected to the same frame. When a breeze blows, each of the parts is affected, turning and twisting by itself. Yet the movement of one part also affects each of the other parts and the mobile as a whole. If someone or something grabs or yanks an individual part, all of the others and the mobile itself would become distorted.

The Family Life Cycle

Pastoral caregivers need to be aware of their own biases in terms of what a "family" looks like. Even families which at one time reflected the *Leave It to Beaver* cultural ideal do not look that way for very long. A typical family begins as a couple, grows as children are added, launches children as they become adults, and returns to the couple in later years. The couple may be joined by one or more of their own parents. Families also may subdivide through divorce, and re-group into stepfamilies. A fairly new twist on family development is the return of adult children to their parents' homes. Family therapists call such change and development within families the "family life cycle."

In terms of adolescent girls, caregivers need to be aware that most of the girls they work with are in families which are in many ways in the midst of one of their most difficult life cycle stages. Families with adolescents are families which are often struggling for identity in the same way the girls are. Parents are having to redefine themselves and their roles; they can no longer exert the control over their daughters' lives that they had previously. They know their daughters are making personal choices without parents' help: the friends they cultivate, the television shows they watch, the music they listen to, their choices for dates. In addition daughters are making decisions about smoking, drinking, using drugs, and/or having sexual relationships. This new freedom is often symbolized in things such as personal telephone lines, "car dates," driver's licenses, youth group overnight trips, and college acceptance letters. As McGoldrick, Heiman, and Carter point out, this is a good time for parents truly to learn the meaning of Niebuhr's "Serenity Prayer": "May I have the ability to accept the things I cannot change, the strength to change the things I can, and the wisdom to know the difference" (McGoldrick, Heiman, and Carter 1993, 426).

Although girls typically will spend less and less time within the family home, and may be more apt to share the intimate details of their lives with friends rather than family members, adolescents also import values *into* the family at this time, bringing new friends, new ideas, and new causes and concerns. The burden for responsible parents is to monitor a girl's "progress"—the responsibility she is able to take for herself, her level of judgment, her control over impulsivity, her ability to resist pressure to be involved in negative activities—and to determine the level of autonomy which is appropriate for her. As parents and youth group leaders know, maturity levels change from day to day; regression is common.

During this life-cycle stage, parents are often struggling through their own identity issues in what is typically called "midlife crisis." Each partner, at this time, re-evaluates his or her own life—career choices, personal choices, and family choices, including the marital relationship. Marriage relationships are often at their rockiest; many couples express the least satisfaction in their marriages during the years in which they are parents of adolescents. This is often a time of intense negotiation over many issues between spouses, including gender roles. Typically men at this point have a desire to turn their energies back to the family,

while many women who have been at home with children are seeking to
venture out (or back out) into the work world or to gain new skills to
begin or advance in their careers.

Pastoral caregivers need to remember that problems they see in adolescent girls may be reflective of the family environments from which
they come. When dealing with a girl's family one should remember that
she is not the only one under stress. The entire family system is being
challenged during this time period. Again, a caregiver's most effective
strategy may be to *normalize* the situation and the tension that everyone is feeling. Normalizing will not remove the root problem, but it
will take some pressure off of the system—members won't have to
worry if they are going crazy on top of all of the other stresses.

In fact, although families with adolescents are notoriously short on
time (and everything else), they are excellent candidates for church-
sponsored support groups. One very creative and daring Christian educator arranged monthly mother-teenage daughter groups which were
held on a rotating basis in member homes. The response from both
mothers and daughters was overwhelming; gathering together in a
nonthreatening environment to hear one another's stories and insights
brought all of the women closer and helped them to know that they
were not alone in their joys or struggles.

Communication Problems

Although pastoral caregivers should never attempt to do family therapy
unless they have received special training and supervision, caregivers
can often be very effective in helping the family to improve communication. Most people think that they are good listeners, but even professional communicators have problems in the midst of stress and conflict.
During a life-cycle stage when everything seems to be falling apart, it is
especially important that family members be able to talk and listen to
one another. Those who work with adolescent girls know that one of
their major complaints about family life is apt to be, "No one listens."
Parents of these girls can become confused by their daughters' interactions with them; many parents resent new sarcasm and cynicism that
have crept into their daughters' repertoires. Both sides can feel as if they
are talking to stone walls.

People want to be understood, especially people who are in the
midst of identity crises—both girls and parents. Listening to someone is
a profound way to show respect. Taking the time to understand what a
girl is saying or feeling is a way of telling her that she matters to you. To

work hard at listening to her is a way of telling her that she is worth getting to know. As Nelle Morton put it so eloquently, if we listen closely we can "hear each other into speech": Listening can give people permission to figure out what it is they want or need to say (1985, 204).

Caregivers can often help family interactions between parents and daughters improve by teaching family members four rather simple rules:

1. Do not blame or accuse. Begin statements of disapproval with the pronoun "I." ("I feel afraid and angry when you come home late" is better than "You are so inconsiderate and irresponsible.")
2. Do not interrupt one another in negative ways (e.g., to change the subject, to drown the other person out). (There are positive interruptions such as words or vocalizations which encourage someone to continue.)
3. Do not assume you know what someone else is thinking. Ask questions to clarify. ("Are you saying that you feel it's unfair when I don't allow you to stay up as late as your older sister?")
4. Do not use the words "never" or "always." ("Please listen to what I have to say; it's important to me," is better than "You never listen to me when I try to talk.")

MORE SERIOUS FAMILY PROBLEMS

Because most family systems problems are very complex, ministers are usually not qualified, nor do they have the time or energy, to work as sole care providers with troubled families. They can, however, do the important work of recognizing the *symptoms* of problems in the people with whom they work, and of helping them to find the kind of professional assistance they need. In best cases, caregivers can make effective referrals of the *entire family* to pastoral counselors or other family therapists.

The most serious problems pastoral caregivers will ever face in families are physical and sexual violence—most often directed toward women, girls, and small children. Incest, the sexual violation of a relatively weak family member by a more powerful family member, will be dealt with in the next chapter. For information on wife-battering and child abuse see Carol Adams's volume in this series, *Woman-Battering* (1994).

There are several other serious family-related problems which pastoral caregivers often encounter with adolescent girls. One of the most frequently seen and easily diagnosed problems is that of *role rigidity*— the (often unconscious) taking of rigid roles by family members in order to protect the family from the effects of its unhealthiness.

Role Rigidity

Every family imposes various roles on its members. Most families could identify, for instance, which member was the "good kid"—the one who could do no wrong—or the "clown"—the one who could make everyone laugh. Some families have "matriarchs" and "patriarchs" who function as centers of family power. In most families, as was noted above, fathers are "breadwinners," and mothers are "hearthkeepers" (whether or not they work outside of the home). Some roles are inherited: a son may become the strong silent one just like his grandfather; a daughter may be the rambunctious hellraiser like her aunt.

In *relatively healthy* families these roles are worn lightly, and with humor; they are not iron-fast; Silent Tom can become crazy Tom if the time is right and he feels that way. Breadwinning Dad can become a rock star at the church talent show. Hearthwarming Mom can also become a marathon runner if she has the desire to. The clown can be unhappy.

In *dysfunctional* families roles are like prison bars which restrict members. In these families—where secrets such as conflict between partners, alcohol or drug abuse, violence, infidelity, neglect, or a combination of these problems affect every aspect of all relationships—the imposed roles mask the family secret and the pain. The clown diverts the family from looking at itself. The silent one is never noticed in all the chaos. The breadwinner feels trapped and too responsible. The hearthwarmer angrily covers over family pain while she suffers inside for herself and for hurting family members. The two roles which youth workers are perhaps most likely to notice in the girls with which they work are at opposite ends of the behavior continuum—the hero/ heroine, who does no wrong, and the scapegoat, who does nothing right.

The Heroine. The family heroine proves to the outside world that the family is good—"How could a bad family produce such a beautiful girl? talented athlete? Phi Beta Kappa? wonderful person?"

None of these good qualities or achievements is negative in itself, obviously. The heroine role is painful because it is so restrictive in dysfunctional families. "Goodness"—not real goodness, but the kind which starves the woman of self-care—is the only element of the heroine's personality which is allowed to develop. Anger and other so-called "bad" feelings are denied and hidden under the surface. Very often heroine girls develop rigid and perfectionistic tendencies; they can't "go with the flow"; they need to control the flow to make sure it ends up where they want it. They lose any sense of spontaneity they may have had as young girls; they become "young fogies"—concerned with law and order—and especially concerned that everything looks good.

For some girls this perfectionism and need for control is even extended to their bodies where anorexia nervosa or bulimia may develop (See Chapter 6). But even those who do not develop eating disorders pay a high price for being heroines. For all their achievement and for all the family honor they bring, they suffer devastating self-esteem losses for two reasons:

1) They begin to think of themselves as commodities, and not as persons deserving of love and respect no matter how they perform. Heroines come to live by the achievement-oriented motto: "You're only as good as your last performance." But their best is never enough. These girls suffer a sense of inevitable futility; they know that no matter how good they are, their families are not being helped. They sense the truth, which is that the family problems are being maintained (or getting worse) because of their stellar behaviors. Anything that takes the pressure off of the real problem (the secret, the abuse, the bad parental relationship) only helps to perpetuate it. These girls become terrified to take risks, because they know they cannot afford to fail.

2) Heroines often develop protective shells around themselves which last their whole lifetimes; they cannot allow people to get to know them. Of all church members the hero/heroine is probably the most convinced of "original sin." Many of them sense that if others became emotionally intimate with them they would be shocked and disgusted at the person hidden behind the perfect exterior.

Heroine girls are often the ones elected to be youth group officers, the ones who run the fund-raisers, and the ones who are quick and capable with most other responsibilities. Caregivers and youth leaders need to be careful in their dealings with these girls that they do not reinforce the family message: "You are the *good* one." "You are the leader." "You are the responsible one." "You are the model for the others." "I wish the other kids would be more like you!" Theologically, these girls need large doses of Luther's exhortation to "sin boldly" (in the knowledge they are redeemed in God's love). If they have wise youth leaders, their youth groups may be the place where they are "off the hook" and able to relax, even encouraged to be adventurous. This change will probably take some coaxing, some patience, and some love.

The Scapegoat. The scapegoat is the focus of family anger—"if only she'd get her life together the family would be fine!" The scapegoat in Lev. 16:20–22 was the goat onto which priests placed the sins of the people on the Day of Atonement, and then set free to carry the sins into the wilderness with it. In families the scapegoat is sacrificed in a similar way; she is sent out to carry the family's sins—to be the one the family can despise. When the scapegoat quits school, or takes drugs, or steals, or ends up in jail, or kills herself, the family feels purged. The evil is out there in her. Ironically, therefore, she is bad for the sake of the family, just as the heroine is good for the family.

A girl who might in other circumstances develop a passion for music, astronomy, French literature, or her faith, is locked into what looks like a passion for bad behavior if she happens to be the family scapegoat. In her family the only identity confirmation she receives is for negative aspects. She often adopts the negative identity which the family has warned her to avoid. (See Chapter 2.)

When caregivers see scapegoats in their churches or youth groups, they are likely to see a curious combination of qualities. Their attention will surely first be drawn to the girl because of her behavior. She may be louder and more disruptive than others. She probably seems to draw trouble to herself—she will find the worst in everyone and bring it to light. She will often encourage others to share in her trouble. It may seem fun and exotic to others—she will be the one who brings cigarettes or beer on field trips; she will be the one sneaking out of the church during lock-ins. But in addition to this bad behavior there may be a vulnerability which is very appealing. In many ways the scapegoat may be the most charismatic and compelling member of the youth group.

The key to dealing with scapegoats is to remember that in spite of their outward demeanor, which is often daredevil or carefree, they are in deep pain. Whereas with heroines caregivers need to permit and encourage some acting up, with scapegoats caregivers need to give permission to act responsibly and well. Scapegoats desperately need someone to see the *good* in them.

Scapegoats are in danger of self-destructing; they often end up with drug, alcohol, or other form of addiction; depression; relationship problems; and problems with the legal system. Some end up suicides.

Unless they are helped somehow to separate from the roles their families have imposed on them, they all too often fulfill their families' predictions about them.

The scapegoat is obviously the family member most likely to be brought in to the youth leader or for counseling. The temptation for caregivers is always to side with the family against the girl, to think that a nice talking to or a little encouragement to act more appropriately would be helpful. A much more effective strategy would be to convince the parents to take part in family therapy. There will almost always be resistance to this idea—after all, the family's strategy is to see the scapegoat as the problem and *not* the family. The brutal truth is that if the girl in front of the caregiver gets well, someone else in the family is *guaranteed* to pick up the bad behavior and become a "problem" if the original unhealthiness in the family is not addressed.

CONCLUSION

Caregivers who want to go to the emotional center of girls' lives usually go to their family relationships. Despite the fact that adolescent girls spend less and less time in their homes, relationships that are growing and changing with both parents and with other family members continue to have profound influence on girls' spiritualities and their psychological wellbeing.

Many times a caregiver will face his or her biggest professional challenges in working with troubled families. Not the least of these challenges is that in looking at other families in pain, one must inevitably look at one's own. Unresolved personal issues with parents, with the family as a whole, or with roles that have tended to follow one into adulthood, often lead caregivers to seek out professional assistance for themselves. This is a sign of health. The goals for the families with which they work, can be claimed by caregivers for their own lives: "You will know the truth, and the truth will make you free."

5

VIOLENCE AGAINST GIRLS

*We're not just a churchgoing family, we have very strong faith
and belief and conviction. So for this to come out was really a
shock. I could not believe what my children were telling me. It
was like watching some wild horror movie. I felt like I wasn't
just in the valley, I was down in the pit.*
  —a mother, Herman and Hirschman, *Father-Daughter Incest*

As this book has mentioned previously, girls and women in this culture
are at risk for being victims of violent sexual and physical abuse.[1] They
are, sadly, most at risk for abuse from men they know, love, and perhaps
even trust. Since 1991 the German journal *Emma* has documented that
the "most dangerous place for Western women is not the street but the
privacy of the home" (Schüssler Fiorenza 1994, ix). Feminist theologian Mary Hunt argues, in fact, that violence is the norm for women,
and justice is only episodic (Brown 1994, 4).

The church all too often has been silent on this danger and the abuse of
women and girls even within church communities. This chapter focuses on
private violence in two forms: incest and dating violence. In each case the
abuse will be described and defined. Common symptoms and consequences
of both will introduced. Girls will often tell caregivers about abuse in nondi-
rect ways; those who work with girls must be constantly aware of the underground messages we are receiving from them, and we must be ready to act to
help girls find safe environments to end the abuse. Although every situation of
abuse is different, some general directions and rules for effective pastoral care
responses will appear at the end of each section.

INCEST

Perhaps the most harmful aspect of the androcentric culture in which
we live is the common but rarely articulated sense that the father in the

family *owns* the other family members, especially the women and children. This belief, which has even been upheld in our legal system, makes some men think that they are entitled to use and abuse family members for their own purposes and gratification. One of the most tragic of these abuses is incest—where a family member, usually male, takes advantage of his power over a weaker member, and coerces her into engaging in sexual acts with him. These acts can be oral, vaginal, or anal intercourse, or they can be fondling, inappropriate caressing, seductive or sexual speech, forcing the child to watch or listen to pornographic materials, forcing a child to watch while the abuser masturbates or has sex with someone else, or making sexual comments about her body.

Unfortunately, abuse of a girl by a father or other male family member is not uncommon in this culture. Studies by sociologists David Finkelhor (1984), Diana Russell (1986), and Gail Wyatt (1985) have revealed that approximately one-third of all girls in this country are sexually abused before the age of eighteen. Of these girls, 89 percent have been abused by a family member (Russell 1986). This means that over 20 million American women and girls have been abused before they reach their eighteenth birthdays, and almost 18 million were abused by a family member whom they should have been able to love and trust (Davies and Frawley 1994, 35).

The figures are even worse for abuse which begins in early childhood. Girls under twelve are the victims of 16 percent of rapes reported to the police; of these victims, 96 percent are raped by relatives or acquaintances, and one in five is raped by her father (U. S. Justice Department 1994). The average age for onset of abuse is six to ten years old (Davies and Frawley 1994, 35). Incest happens to girls who attend church and youth groups, and it is happening to girls we know all the time.

The Necessity of Reporting

The first thing caregivers need to remember about incest is: it is a sin against God and the victim, and a gross betrayal of trust and power. It is *never* the victim's fault. Also, despite some traditional psychotherapeutic views, it is not the *mother's* fault. Responsibility for the act of abuse lies squarely and only with the abuser.

Next, caregivers need to understand that incest is a criminal act. In many states clergy are legally required to report incest or suspected incest to law enforcement or child protection agencies.[2] In most cases laws are designed to require certain categories of persons to report suspected abuse within a given time frame. These informants are then generally exempted from civil or criminal liability as long as the report is made in good faith. A person may be subject to criminal penalties for failure to make a report. Churches and caregivers need to take responsibility to know what requirements are for their own states.[3]

Whether or not it is a minister's legal responsibility to report abuse or suspected abuse, it is the minister/caregiver's *ethical* responsibility to report any form of child abuse. Caregivers often understand themselves to be agents of healing and restoration in human relationships, and they are often very uncomfortable with the idea of reporting abuse because they know the turmoil it will cause. It is necessary and realistic in cases of abuse, however, to remember that filing a report is not *causing* the conflict; the *abuse* causes the turmoil and pain. Ministers are also taught to protect family privacy. In cases of abuse, however, priorities need to shift in order to ensure the safety of the children involved and to stop the abuse from continuing.[4]

Theologically, Matthew 18:5–6 and the words of Jesus give ministers a mandate to act and protect children:

> Whoever welcomes one such child in my name welcomes me; but if any of you put a stumbling block before one of these little ones who believe in me, it would be better for you if a great millstone were fastened around your neck and you were drowned in the depth of the sea.

Jesus was a champion of the powerless; he unfailingly offered comfort, healing, and attention to those the culture would have despised. He healed the outcast woman with the issue of blood; he accepted passionate tributes from women who were disreputable to their communities; and he refused to allow his disciples to shuffle the children to the background. These were the vulnerable ones: the ones with no power or prestige; the ones that would not have a claim to attention or justice without his blessing, validation, and protection.

In addition to making sure the abuser is stopped, a report of abuse can be the first step toward healing for the victim. Incest is such a horrendous violation and does such deep injury to children that survivors often need many years of intensive therapy, even after they are in safe environments and away from their abusers. Abusers also need therapy that holds them responsible for actions and teaches them about abusive power relationships. Other family members also are hurt by incest, and they usually need some form of therapy.

Once the decision to report has been made, there are several categories of professionals to which ministers should consider turning in order to ensure the girl's *safety* and to begin the healing process for her and her family:

1. First, a minister needs to contact law enforcement or child protection agencies. He or she may wish to consult an attorney before doing this to make sure that every legal means possible is used to protect the girl. Ideally, ministers will have made contact with agencies *before* they become aware of any specific abuse, and will have become acquainted with an administrator responsible for supervising caseworkers. Case workers, as well intentioned as they may be, are often overwhelmed with unmanageable case loads, and they may not be able to give full attention to the girl being brought to them for help.

2. Second, ministers usually have input into families even after abuse has been reported. In concert with the child protection agencies (which become the primary "case managers" after abuse has been reported) ministers can suggest professional counselors for the girl, and separate counselors for her mother and the abuser. It is *never* a good idea for girls and their abusers to do joint therapy or family therapy immediately after abuse is reported. Joint or family therapy tends to focus on *relationships* and to spread responsibility for problems evenly across family members. Abuse is one instance where thinking in terms of family systems is not helpful—at least initially. Before relational issues are explored, responsibility needs to be established clearly with the abuser, and safety issues must be addressed. Abused girls are not partners in bad relationships; they are victims of abuses of power. Abusers need to take full responsibility for their abuse and to experience whatever consequences the church and legal authorities deem appropriate.

As Marie Fortune advises:
The goals of any effective response to abuse should follow this order:

1. Protect the child from further abuse.
2. Stop the abuser's violence.
3. Heal the victim's brokenness and, if [this is] possible, restore the family relationships; if [it is] not possible, mourn the loss of that relationship.[4]

Why a Victim Stays Silent

As stated above, girls do not often come directly to ministers or care-givers to talk about incest or sexual abuse. There are multiple reasons for this. Primarily, girls do not speak directly because they are afraid. An abuser has many ways of keeping his victim in enforced silence because of the power he has in his family:

1. Abusers are physically larger than their victims and can threaten them with physical harm. Children learn very early (by being picked up and carried when they were infants, for instance) that they have very little power to resist adults. Girls often resort to running away from home because they believe it is the only way to resist abuse by adults (Janus et al. 1987, 101–102).
2. Abusers threaten girls with the consequences of what will happen if the abuse is reported—that they will be taken away from their families, that the abuser will go to jail, that their families would be separated, or that no one would believe them.
3. Abusers threaten to hurt other people or pets. Victims believe that by not telling authorities about the abuse they are protecting loved ones. One woman described the threat she received when she was a child:
   The worst memory is when I told him I was going to tell Mom what he was doing, and he said if I did he would kill her and chop her into little bits. As I child I believed he would do this, and by not telling anyone I felt as if I was protecting her in some way (La Fontaine, 78).
4. Some victims believe that by taking the abuse on themselves they are sparing their sisters or mother from abuse. They are often very serious about this protective role: One minister reports that a member of his youth group confided in him that she had tried to poison her father's morning coffee with rat killer before she went to church and was disappointed that he was still alive when she got home. The minister later discovered that the girl had been sexually abused by her father for many years. She was about to leave home to go to college, and she did not want her younger sister to be abused when she left.
5. Abusers have financial power over their victims. Some victims will not report abuse because they know their families would suffer severe financial loss if their fathers lost employment or went to jail.
6. Some victims refuse to disclose abuse because of a feeling of love and loyalty to the abuser: "I loved my father so much. I respected

him as a father. But I was confused, didn't understand. I wanted it
to stop. I hated that part of it so much" (La Fontaine, 79).

7. Many victims are ignorant of the fact that what their abusers are
doing is wrong. They know that they do not like being abused, but
abuse feels normal to them in their families. Their fathers may explain abuse to them in what seems like a rational way: "All fathers
do this to their girls, but no one talks about it."

8. Abusers try to keep their victims isolated from social support systems.

9. Victims feel guilty and responsible, and especially do not want their
mothers to know about the abuse.

10. Victims do not trust authorities to listen to them, understand
them, or act in ways that would not endanger them further.

Rather than to disclose abuse, many victims go to great lengths to try to
protect themselves from it. Strategies include: wearing many layers of
clothing to thwart the abuser's hands, arranging schedules so as never
to be alone at home with the abuser, and trying always to be in the
company of a friend or sibling when in the presence of the abuser.

Symptoms of Incest and Abuse

Caregivers need to be alert and sensitive to symptoms of abuse which
may be exhibited in youth group members. One minister in a small
rural church said that a young teenager came up to her after a church
breakfast and secretly handed her a folded up napkin. When the minister looked at it later, she saw that the girl had written a note: "To God
and Jesus" on the outside of the napkin. When she opened it up she saw
the words, "Why can't me and my brother live with our real Ma?" The
next day, knowing something about the girl's circumstances and sus-
pecting that the girl was trying to tell her about abuse, the minister
made a point of calling on the girl at her high school. The girl, in tears,
told her that her grandfather, with whom she was living, had begun
molesting her.

Other signs of abuse may be even more unobtrusive—depression,
continuing problems in school, signs of self-abuse such as scratches on
forearms or ankles, signs of drug abuse, signs of personal distress (e.g.,
wearing only black, wearing severe makeup, etc.), and talking about
wanting to die or to run away from home. Table 1 gives a list of symptoms which are often seen along with sexual abuse.

Besides the physical trauma, girls who are abused suffer severe emotional trauma; they are often in extreme psychological peril. If their abuse

Table 1
Adolescent Symptoms of Sexual Abuse

Continued School Problems
Noninvolvement in extracurricular activities
Truancy
Fear of speaking in class

Continued Physical Complaints

Menstrual Problems
Shame or fear about menses
Severe cramps
Depression during menses
Pain or fear while inserting a tampon
Inability to insert a tampon because of vaginal muscle contractions

Weight or Body Image Problems
Excessive weight gain at puberty
Discomfort with and disgust about the body
Embarrassment or disgust at the development of secondary sex characteristics
Distorted view of body, especially of stomach as huge or bulging

Anorexia or Bulimia

Continued Sleep Disturbances

Problems with Sex/Intimacy
Promiscuity
Prostitution
Adolescent pregnancy
Adolescent marriage
Complete avoidance of boys and dating

Impulsive Behavior
Running away
Drug and alcohol abuse
Self-mutilation
Stealing

Suicidal Ideation, Suicide Attempts

From: Jody Messler Davies & Mary Gail Frawley, *Treating the Adult Survivor of Childhood Sexual Abuse: A Psychoanalytic Perspective*, New York: Basic Books, 1994, p. 38.

is repeated, the damage to them is comparable to that of soldiers who have been in intense warfare over a long period of time. Judith Herman, a psychiatrist, believes that abused girls suffer not only from the abuse but from the craziness and arbitrariness of the abusive situation:

> The child trapped in an abusive environment is faced with formidable tasks of adaptation. She must find a way to preserve a sense of trust in people who are untrustworthy, safety in a situation that is unsafe, control in a situation that is terrifyingly unpredictable, power in a situation of helplessness (1992, 96).

Girls who have been abused report terror of the threats made by their abusers and also powerlessness in the face of these threats. They are aware emotionally, even if they have not named it cognitively, that their homes are crazy; lies are common and secrets are well kept. They often develop acute sensitivities to their environments and learn to be always on guard and constantly alert. Victims become especially attuned to their abusers' emotional states, and will stay vigilant for any signs of an impending attack. Girls describe listening for footsteps outside their bedroom doors at night, watching their abusers' eyes constantly during their waking hours for the look that means an attack is immanent, and praying that abusers will drink themselves to sleep. These girls pay close attention, and they see everything. Often their hyperattention becomes second nature and out of their conscious control. Hypervigilance becomes their normal mode of being.

Two other emotional states are common to abused girls: an almost compulsive need to please and a powerful sense of abandonment. Abused girls know that their homes are totally unpredictable and arbitrary. When this knowledge is coupled with the constant threat of violence and death by their abusers, girls look for any possible way to gain control or safety. They often come to believe that the ability to make people happy is their only means of protection. They will go to extravagant lengths to try to be good, hoping thereby to forestall attacks on themselves and others.

During the time girls are being abused, they also wonder where responsible adults are in their world. Their abusers are obviously not protecting them from harm, but neither are the other members of their family or social system. If caregivers learn about or have good reasons to suspect incest or abuse, it is imperative that they *act* on this knowledge. If they do not act, they will become further examples of the many untrustworthy adults that abused girls can add to their lists. If a girl tells a caregiver about incest, she is giving a sacred responsibility to protect her and her life. She may never tell anyone else.

Providing a Safe Environment

In addition to being attentive to symptoms and signs of abuse in girls, caregivers need to provide safe environments for them while they are at church or with the youth group. A safe environment means many things, but most of all it means protection from sexual and physical abuse from the caregiver, from other adult members of the youth team, and from other members of the youth group. In a safe environment a girl can tell a caregiver about abuse (even if she does not name it as such) knowing that the caregiver will listen, believe, and respond appropriately.

> In an event planning session with the senior high youth fellowship, Gary, one of the adult sponsors, kept pushing for a hay ride, even though some of the girls adamantly opposed the idea. The minister in charge of the evening could not understand what was going on, but sensed it was something important. He approached the girls after the meeting. They told him that on hay rides Gary liked to stuff hay up the girls' sweaters. They also did not want to have pool parties if Gary was going to be present, because he liked to grab them and throw them in the pool. The minister promptly removed Gary from the youth team.

In addition to being alert and sensitive to signs of abuse by others toward the girls in their care, caregivers must be aware of their own power over members of the youth group and the responsibilities and constraints that come with that power. A minister or adult sponsor is older, has access to the power structures of the church, may have more physical strength, and has the power of his or her position—entrusted with the care of youth by the church and God. Ministers are viewed as real connections to the holy by youth and other church members. This situation means that any form of sexual relationship with a youth group member is strictly forbidden. A youth group member cannot engage in a mutual relationship with someone who is so much older and has so much more power than he or she has. This situation is true even if the youth seems to be initiating a relationship or consenting to one that is offered.

Sexuality is a good gift of God and is a part of all human interaction. Indeed, it gives energy, creativity, and a spirit of excitement to life. It is very natural for caregivers and youth group leaders to *feel* sexually attracted to young people. It is always wrong, however, to *act* on those feelings. Peter Rutter, a physician, describes what he considers the forbidden zone of sexuality: "a condition of relationship in which sexual behavior is prohibited because a [person in power] holds in trust the intimate, wounded, vulnerable, or undeveloped parts of a woman [or girl]" (1989, 28).[5] What constitutes abusive behavior in the forbidden zone with girls? Anything that would deprive them of their dignity, power, and individual boundaries. A real sense of personal boundaries, which tell a girl where she leaves off and the world begins, is often just being formed in adolescence. Girls are trained to please others and not to say no. This training makes them easy targets for abusers. Ministers should help girls to understand their rights and authority over their own bodies and psyches by making sure never to invade a girl's boundaries. Invasions can take the form of touching a girl's body (with or without erotic intent), touching oneself erotically in view of the girl; "accidentally" brushing up against a girl (as Gary did in the illustration above), speaking suggestively to a girl or telling off-color jokes in her presence, or making comments about a girl's body or appearance. Invasions can also take the form of inappropriate emotional intimacy. It is never permissable to share intimate details of an adult's life with a child or young person; girls should not be burdened with knowledge of a caregiver's marriage or emotional or personal state. Adults should share adult problems with other adults.

Prevention

Realistically, because most incestuous abuse begins when a girl is between six and ten years old, ministers will not be able to prevent incest in adolescents' homes by training the adolescents. Caregivers who are pastors need to include the topic of abuse as a part of the teaching agenda for the entire church. Parents, especially fathers, need to be taught that, according to the gospel, they do not *own* their families. Children are to be respected as individuals and as co-members of the Body of Christ. Children, especially girls, need to be taught that they have a right to say no when they are being violated, even by those they love, and that they need to tell trustworthy adults if they are being hurt. Children can be taught that abuse is not their fault. They can also be taught to resist manipulation by adults and to recognize behaviors which signify abuse. Table 2 is a list of these kinds of behaviors compiled from a group of children who had been abused.

The struggle against sexual abuse and incest is an extremely difficult one for at least two reasons: (1) The culture (including churches) tends to be in denial that a problem exists, and (2) one of the culture's most cherished but unexamined values is that a man's home is his castle and his wife and children are his property. For ministers to *name* the prob-

Table 2
Behaviors That Signify Abuse

Here are some things that children who have been sexually abused said other children could be on the lookout for.

Treating you differently from other kids: Treating you better than other kids, or being meaner to you. Wanting to spend time alone with you. Making excuses to go places or have others leave. Not letting you have friends or do things that other kids your age do.

Treating you as if you were an adult: Telling you private things, about his wife/your mother. Saying you are different, special, the only one who really understands. Telling you that you are better than his wife. Or, acting like a kid when he's with you.

Violating your personal space or your privacy: Asking you to do things that involve physical contact, like giving backrubs or washing his back. Accidently-on-purpose brushing against your breasts or crotch while wrestling, rubbing his body against yours. Looking at or touching your body and saying it's just to see how you are developing. Putting lotion or ointment on you when there is nothing wrong with you or when your mother or others aren't around. Coming into your room while you are undressed or into the bathroom when you're in there. Not letting you close your bedroom door or the bathroom door. Coming into your bedroom at night. Walking around naked, or accidently-on-purpose letting his robe come apart.

Bribes and secrecy: Giving you special privileges or favors and making you feel obligated. Telling you not to tell your mother or other people about things that happen between you.

Inappropriate talk: Asking questions or making accusations about sexual relations between you and your boy or girlfriend. Teaching "sex education" by showing pornographic pictures, showing you his body or touching your body. Saying sexual things to you about the way you dress. Talking to you about the sexual things he has done.

From: Karen Adams and Jennifer Fay, *Helping Your Child Recover From Sexual Abuse*, Seattle: University of Washington Press, 1987, p. 12.

lem and to *attack* the value is to "take on" the structure of the environment of which they are a part and in which they labor. Not many people can do this work alone. It is a very good idea to build up support networks of likeminded professionals, especially likeminded clergy, to fortify each other for the inevitable battles which will ensue.

DATING VIOLENCE

Girls in this culture are taught that heterosexual dating, at its best, is a romantic adventure. Girls' magazines are filled with images of handsome young men, beautiful flowers, dinners for two, holding hands, and tender secrets. The reality for girls too many times is vastly different from their expectations. Dates and dating relationships can and often do become nightmares of violence.

> Shauna came to church school looking bedraggled and tired. She slept through most of the hour, with her head on her arms on the table. She didn't move when the class was dismissed, and remained in her seat after her classmates had left. Joanna, her teacher, joked, "It's time to go, if you can get yourself awake enough to leave."
>
> Shauna raised her head, and Joanna could see there were tears in her eyes. Joanna sat down to see if Shauna wanted to talk. After a few minutes Shauna told her about the previous evening: she had gone to a party with a boy she had been seeing seriously for several months. They had gotten into an argument when she wanted to leave the party early. They went out to the driveway, and he hit her several times on the back and arms.
>
> She had no visible bruises, but when she rolled up her blouse sleeves, Joanna was horrified by the welts and discoloration. Shauna began crying, "I couldn't sleep last night I was so scared and sore. I can't believe he'd do this to me."

Some studies of dating or acquaintance violence have estimated that if physical abuse is defined as: "the use or threat of physical force or restraint that has the purpose of causing injury or pain to another individual" then approximately 25 percent of girls on college campuses have been physically abused by someone with whom they were in a dating relationship (Sugarman and Hotaling 1991, 104).

In addition to physical injuries that a girl sustains from violence in a dating relationship, she also sustains emotional injury. Women outnumber men by almost three to one for those instances in which severe emotional trauma was the outcome of a violent incident (Sugarman and Hotaling, 105–107). The most common emotional aftereffects on an adolescent victim of violence are: sudden personality changes; a drop in school performance; withdrawal from school or peer group activities (such as youth group); promiscuous sexual behavior; sudden phobic behaviors (such as intense fears of public places [including church], fears of driving, fears of losing control); drug or alcohol abuse; self-destructive behavior; and development of eating disorders (Hilberman 1976).

In everyday terms, a girl who has been violently abused by a dating partner will probably lose her ability to take part in her normal world. For adolescents violence and rape are even more devastating than for adult women. Adolescent girls lose first, that important and precious newly developing sense of who they are, the sense of wholeness and integrity that they are struggling to achieve or maintain. Second, they lose the sense that they have any control over their bodies or their environments. One young girl reported that she "gave up the hope that anything would be stable or normal in my life" after an attack. Third, a rape of an adolescent girl does serious damage to her sense of her own sexuality. She may not at this point be able clearly to distinguish whether or not she consented to having sex with an attacker, and future sexual encounters may be tinged with a feeling of being violated. Finally, teenagers are self-centered naturally, and are therefore much more likely to blame themselves for an attack than an adult woman might be (Gallers and Lawrence 1991, 174–175).

In addition, some victims of violence report post-traumatic stress disorder symptoms including: the re-experience of the trauma in dreams, intrusive and intense memories, or sudden emotions; emotional numbing; hyperalertness; sleep problems; survival guilt; problems with memory or concentration; and avoidance of activities which remind the victim of the abuse.

Caregiver Response

As with incest, the single most important step a caregiver can take when he or she learns that a girl has been or is continuing to be abused by someone she knows, is to move to ensure her safety. While no caregiver ever wants to betray a girl's confidence, if a caregiver suspects or knows of abuse, it is his or her *ethical* mandate to assist the girl (especially a young adolescent) in reporting it to those who are responsible for her safety, or to others who can facilitate a safe environment for her.

If a girl comes to a caregiver in a crisis situation, as Shauna did above, immediately after an incident of violence has taken place, the following steps should be taken:

1. Reassure the girl that the incident was not her fault. Nothing she could have done, including drinking, taking drugs, kissing or making out with her date, or parking in a deserted area with him, authorized him to hit her or rape her. Let the girl know that you believe her. If the caregiver is male he should immediately contact a woman to be with him and the girl during this time.
2. If she is under eighteen years old, contact her parents or guardians to let them know she is in your presence and safe, but that an abuse has taken place. Offer them the opportunity to join you, if the girl feels this presence is safe. It is important to remember that a girl's family often plays a very important part in her recovery (or nonrecovery) from abuse. In families with very rigid roles, girls who are abused may be treated differently according to the roles they are assigned. It is, for instance, especially crucial to guard against any family response to scapegoat girls which may indicate that the girl is being blamed for her own victimization.
3. After obtaining parents' permission (if she is under eighteen) take her to the nearest rape crisis center or to a hospital or medical facility so that she can be examined for injury and so that evidence of rape, other sexual abuse, or other physical violence can be gathered. Ask the parents to meet you there. Make sure that the girl does not bathe or "clean up" before she is seen by medical professionals.
4. See to it that the girl is taken seriously by the medical professionals who treat her and law enforcement officials who may question her or speak with her. Doctors should make the girl feel as comfortable as possible. They should document the emotional state of the girl and the form of abuse that took place. They should also document any physical injury or signs of sexual assault.
5. Help the parents to find a therapist for the girl and a support group if possible. Parents also will often need help dealing with their daughter's abuse, as they often experience great anger accompanied by a sense of helplessness. These feelings, like the girl's, often continue for many months or years.
6. Be available to discuss whether or not the girl and her parents wish to bring legal charges against the abuser. Often this discussion will be initiated at the rape crisis center or medical setting. Girls and their parents may need to hear your reassurance that forgiving an abuser may not be possible for a long time, if ever. In any case, forgiveness does not mean absolving people's responsiblity for their abusive actions.
7. Let the girl and her family know that you will not desert them as they work through the healing process, that you will be there for

emotional and spiritual support if they wish it. Especially, let them know, when the time is right, that it is normal and appropriate to be angry with God at times like these.

Prevention of Dating Violence

The most important aspect of preventing dating violence may be education of both girls and boys as to the meaning of bodily integrity and mutual consent for sexual behavior. Adolescents who have grown up in a culture in which video game action represents torture and murder, and in which homicides and assaults are common fare on television, can be desensitized to violence and violent behavior. In addition, many children have been spanked or hit as forms of discipline (some by parents who believe this is biblically mandated) and have watched their mothers be abused by their fathers. Among the messages they may have received from this exposure to violence is: (1) that it is normal, and (2) that it is appropriate for some kinds of situations.

These children and young adults need to be taught that (1) physical violence on their part is never appropriate behavior, and (2) if they are abused it is never their fault. There is never an *excuse* to hit someone they are dating, and their dates never have an excuse to hit them. In addition, adolescents need to relearn appropriate sexual behaviors. Men and boys need to learn to view forced sex (rape) for what it is and to work to stop it on a personal and societal level. Women need to stop blaming themselves for rape but also to learn to say no in ways that are as clearly understandable as possible by the men they are with. In this culture men often believe that when a woman says no she means she does not want to be seen as enjoying sex too much or being too easy. Some men have claimed that they forced a woman to have sex because they believed she really wanted to engage in sexual acts, but she did not want to lose her reputation.

In 1981 two researchers asked 106 college students, who responded anonymously, about their beliefs concerning dating behavior. The men who responded rated intercourse against the woman's wishes as significantly more justifiable when the woman initiated the date, when the man paid, and when the couple went to the man's apartment (Muehlenhard and McFall 1981). These beliefs can lead to victimization of girls. Both boys and girls need to know that there is never a time when forced sex (intercourse or other types) is appropriate. Girls never owe sex to a boy; no always means no.

Both boys and girls also need to know that there are identified risk factors for date rape. These include:

1. the male's initiating and taking a dominant role during the date;
2. miscommunication between the couple regarding sex;
3. heavy alcohol or drug use that reduces a man's inhibitions and a woman's ability to consent or to refuse
4. parking or going to other isolated situations; and
5. male acceptance of
   a. traditional sex roles,
   b. interpersonal violence,
   c. adversarial attitudes in relationships, and
   d. the above cultural myths about rape (that women really want it) (Muehlenhard and Linton 1987).

Both girls and boys can learn to avoid situations which are risky according to the above criteria. In particular, girls should learn that they can protect themselves best if they are not under the influence of alcohol and drugs. Each partner on a date has rights which are not to be violated: to be respected, to be mutually responsible for planning, and to refuse behaviors that are uncomfortable or that violate their belief systems.

CONCLUSION

Becoming aware of and becoming active in the battle against incest, sexual abuse of children, and dating violence is a difficult task. It can force caregivers to look carefully at their own families and their own values, a process which requires a deep level of courage and faith. Responding to a disclosure of incest or violence can call into question many of the matters that caregivers believe and cherish about their roles as ministers, especially that they should be peacemakers and not instigators of crisis. It cannot be said too often, however, that a minister who believes a girl about abuse and responds appropriately is not provoking crisis—the abuser did that. A minister who reports abuse or violence, attempts to ensure the victim's safety, and directs her toward a path of healing is embodying Christ's love toward her. A minister who teaches his or her congregation about abuse and who prepares children to resist coercive power and claim their own emotional and bodily rights, lays a foundation for safety, health, and salvation for many generations to come.

6

SPECIAL PROBLEMS

Question #4: Would you rather:
Get run over by a truck (54.3 percent)
Gain 150 pounds (42.9 percent)
—from the *Esquire* Poll on the
State of American Womanhood

Up to this point there has been very little discussion of the bodies of adolescent girls, the development of which signals the onset of adolescence. The truth is that while *young* girls often see their bodies as good or OK, *older* girls often think of their bodies as problems.

Question 21 on the Spirituality Questionnaire asks girls to describe their feelings about their bodies. Of the seventeen eleven- and twelve-year-olds who answered the question, fifteen were totally positive ("I think it's special because God made it." "I think my body is beautiful." "I think my body is nice looking.") and one was mixed: "I think my body is fat and God's."

From the seventeen- and eighteen-year-olds who answered the question, however, there was a much more guarded or even negative tone to the responses: "I think my body is ?" "I try to be happy about my body—sometimes this is hard for me." "I think my body is average, I need to work out a little more often." "I think my body is fine, but I always can find plenty of things wrong with it." "I think my body is a little overweight, mostly because of pressure from my skinny mother. My big breasts are an advantage for attraction, but I'm getting sick of it." Finally, "I think my body is not proportioned well and has *much* room for improvement." By late adolescence these girls seemed to have learned an important, but negative, cultural lesson. Their bodies are not their own. There seems to be a standard—set by mothers, (who often feel they must make their daughters marriageable) by men, or by something else out there—to which they need to conform.

Their bodies are *objects* for them to mold, manipulate, and use to their best advantage.

This chapter deals with three special problems of adolescent girls. Two have to do specifically with girls' bodies: eating disorders and sexual problems. The third, depression, has to do with the sense of hopelessness girls feel about their bodies, lives, and possibilities. Because pastoral caregivers rarely have the training or time to deal with such complicated issues in depth, this chapter is in the form of a first aid manual. A problem will be described and defined; normal symptoms will be given; and referral strategies will be discussed. In especially complicated cases, pastoral interventions—bringing the problem to the notice of parents and health professionals—may be necessary. Suggestions for these interventions are included.

EATING DISORDERS

Eating disorders are basically of two types: *anorexia nervosa*, characterized by the fear of becoming obese and the subsequent refusal to eat, and *bulimia,* characterized by fear of obesity, recurrent episodes of binge eating which may be followed by purging (vomiting or using diet pills, diuretics, or laxatives) or periods of self-starvation.

Both anorexia and bulimia are potentially deadly disorders. Up to 5 percent of those who are diagnosed with anorexia eventually die from the disease. Although the figures are not as clear with bulimia, it is probable that it also can lead to death (Hsu 1990, 192). The average age of onset of anorexia is seventeen years; of bulimia is eighteen years. Most studies show that between 1 percent and 2 percent of women in this country and Western Europe are anorectic, and between 2 percent and 4.5 percent are bulimic (Hsu 1990, 22, 65). This means for every one hundred girls, between three and six have severe problems with eating or noneating.

Both disorders are disease categories in the *Diagnostic and Statistical Manual of Mental Disorders-IV (DSM-IV)*, the guidebook for standardized diagnosis developed by the American Psychiatric Association (1994).[1]

Anorexia Nervosa

The *DSM-IV* diagnostic criteria for anorexia nervosa includes:

A. Refusal to maintain body weight over a minimal normal weight for age and height.

B. Intense fear of gaining weight or becoming fat, even though underweight.
C. Disturbance in the way in which one's body weight, size, or shape is experienced, e.g., the person claims to feel fat even when emaciated, believes that one area of the body is too fat even when obviously underweight.
D. In females, absence of at least three consecutive menstrual cycles when otherwise expected to occur.[2]

The girl with anorexia nervosa is extremely afraid that she will become, or that she is, fat. In addition, she is often preoccupied with food and its preparation, although she may refuse to eat, or she may only eat very small portions. She often has no sense that she is starving herself; even when she is pathetically thin, she feels fat.

One study of girls with anorexia who had been hospitalized in England found that they had highly developed strategies for avoiding eating (even while in treatment) including: hiding food in their napkins; leaving a crust of bread or toast on their plates and discarding the rest; hiding food in vases, stuffed toys, cupboards, and on window ledges; storing food in their mouths until they could spit it out while brushing their teeth; and, feeding family pets under the table (Abraham and Llewellyn-Jones 1992, 91).

Bulimia Nervosa

In the *DSM-IV*, a diagnosis of bulimia nervosa is made based on the following criteria:

A. Recurrent episodes of binge eating (e.g., rapid consumption of a large amount of food in a relatively short period of time and with a feeling of lack of control over the eating during these episodes).
B. A recurring use of inappropriate compensatory behavior (e.g., self-induced vomiting, use of laxatives or diuretics, strict dieting or fasting, or vigorous exercise) in order to prevent weight gain.
D. A minimum of two binge eating and compensatory behavior episodes a week for 3 months.
E. Body shape and weight unduly influence self-evaluation.

A girl is not considered bulimic if these behaviors occur only during episodes of anorexia nervosa.[3]

The girl who has bulimia feels a consistent and overpowering urge to overeat, usually in connection with some stress or problem which has arisen in her life. This overeating, or binge eating, however intensifies her stress by producing feelings of lack of control—that the eating could neither be avoided, nor terminated once it began. About 60 percent of binge-eaters take diet pills with laxatives in them; about 40 percent take diuretics (Abraham & Llewellyn-Jones, 1992, 110). Based on a 1992 study of what constitutes binge eating, Spitzer et al. suggested that a binge eating disorder was characterized by eating more in a short period of time than most other people would eat; feeling a lack of control while eating; eating more rapidly than normal and until feeling uncomfortably full; eating large amounts of food when not feeling hungry; eating throughout the day with no planned mealtimes; eating alone from embarrassment; and feeling disgusted, guilty, or depressed after overeating.

There is little agreement among mental health professionals about what *causes* eating disorders. Some believe that they are based in biochemical processes. Some believe that they are based in family dynamics (the girl struggling to keep the family together over her problem, or to gain power and attention in the family). Most feminists believe that they are caused by social/cultural pressures on girls and women to be thin (Bordo 1993; Woodman 1980; Miles 1994). In all probability, all three factors come into play to produce anorexia or bulimia. There is little doubt that eating disorders are, in addition to the other factors, in some way related to the cultural standard for women's bodies. This standard has gotten smaller and thinner since the 1950s, when a voluptuous woman like Marilyn Monroe was considered ideal. All professionals agree that eating disorders are emotionally painful for a girl and for her family, and are extremely dangerous to a girl's health.

There are definite patterns in the kinds of girls who have anorexia and bulimia. They tend to be perfectionistic, and very hard on themselves; they tend toward dichotomous thinking: good/evil and fat/thin (Garfinkel & Garner 1982). These girls also tend toward rigid thinking about sex roles and familial obligations (Striegel-Moore, Silberstein, & Rodin 1986). Behind their perfect exteriors they are likely to have extreme feelings of inferiority and powerlessness. Girls with bulimia also have problems with impulse control.

Families of girls with eating disorders tend to be perfectionistic, high-achieving and intolerant of conflict. They are often unable to accept differences in family members and resent members who try to

strike out on their own. These families tend to be rather cold and focused on the needs of the parents over the children (Garfinkel and
Garner 1982). Power struggles over a girl's eating are common.

Caregiver Response

Caregivers usually will not have access to information about how, what,
or when girls are eating. Generally, they can suspect an eating disorder
when family members of a girl come to them for help or when they
notice a girl who is particularly thin and perhaps unhealthy looking.
This girl may be exercising more than normal and may not be eating
dinners or snacks with the rest of the youth group (or may be pretend-
ing to eat and hiding the fact that she is not). At advanced stages of
eating disorders, when a girl is extremely emaciated, she will become
very sensitive to hot and cold; her hands and feet may feel cold to the
touch and may look bluish; her skin will be dry and her hair brittle; and
a soft downy hair may appear on her face, back, or arms.

When a family brings a girl with a suspected eating disorder to a caregiver, he or she should listen carefully. Most often there will be signs of
intense conflict over the girl's eating; the girl will often deny the problem exists. Unless a parent is clearly mistaken, a caregiver can suggest a
medical evaluation with a physician who is familiar with eating disorders
and adolescent girls. (To find a physician such as this, caregivers might
consider calling dietary therapists in their areas to find out where they
send their clients.)

If for some reason the family is unable to locate such a physician or
wishes to try to admit the girl to treatment immediately, the caregiver
should be able to provide some criteria to help families judge whether
or not a specific program has the components needed to make it as effective as possible.

1. The program could be inpatient or outpatient, unless a girl is obviously at a very advanced level of her disease, in which case, she
   should be admitted on an inpatient basis, so nutrients can be administered.
2. The program should be medically directed, e.g., there should be a
   physician who will take primary or supervisory responsibility for a
   girl's care.
3. The program should be staffed by licensed therapists.
4. The program should be able to give information about outcomes
   (i.e., how well girls do in the program, and how recovery is measured).

5. The program should include consultation by a licensed or certified dietary therapist.
6. The program should have a strong education component that will teach girls about their disease, about nutrition and healthy eating, and about coping behaviors.
7. The program should have a strong *family* component, where family members are required to attend education and counseling sessions with the girl.
8. The program should incorporate Twelve-Step programs, especially Overeaters Anonymous (OA) as part of their treatment. (People with anorexia also attend OA.)
9. The program should have a strong aftercare component, so that a girl and her family are not left alone when she graduates.
10. Finally, the program should recognize the caregiver's importance in the healing process. Eating disorders, in addition to being physical and emotional diseases, are also diseases of the spirit. Girls will need help often to redefine God—Where is God in their struggle? What kind of help will God give?

DEPRESSION

Studies which reflect the differences between genders in terms of incidence of depression show that from adolescence (age thirteen or fourteen) until old age (age sixty-five), girls and women are much more depressed than men (Kashani et al. 1987; Myers et al. 1984). In adolescence 13.3 percent of girls and only 2.7 percent of boys are depressed. In addition, adolescent girls attempt suicide much more often than boys (Petzel and Riddle 1981); boys' attempts, however, are more successful than girls' attempts.

Although significantly more attention is being paid in recent years to chronic depression in both adults and adolescents, many people, including caregivers, often have a tendency to underestimate the effects and pain of depression on affected individuals. People who have not been depressed often make the mistake of equating depression with their own transitory periods of unhappiness. In addition, people who are depressed often do not *look* sick; there are no wounds or blood and no bacteria or virus. Depressed people can seem to be functioning well. It is important to note, however, that depressed people can't shake it off or whistle a happy tune and get over it. Many people who are depressed talk about feeling as if they are walking around in a gray fog; their bodies may seem heavy and hard to move; their thoughts are often confused and dull; they cannot see beyond the immediate moment; and their lives feel empty and worthless.

The *DSM-IV* criteria for a major depressive episode include the following: (For a diagnosis of depression #1 or #2 has to be present, along with four other signs.)

1. Depressed mood (or irritable mood for children and adolescents) most of the day nearly every day.
2. Loss of interest or pleasure in all, or almost all, activities most of the day, nearly every day.
3. Significant weight loss or weight gain when not dieting, or decrease or increase in appetite nearly every day.
4. Sleep problems (too little, too much, problems falling asleep, or staying asleep).
5. Being hyper or lethargic every day.
6. Fatigue or loss of energy every day.
7. Feelings of worthlessness or excessive inappropriate guilt.
8. Inability to think, concentrate, or make decisions.
9. Recurrent thoughts of death, thinking about suicide, wishes to be dead, or suicide attempts.[4]

In addition, there are signs of depression which are specific to adolescents. These include motor retardation, sleeping longer than is normal for the individual, and delusions.[5] They also may include negativistic or antisocial behaviors such as: (1) deterioration of school performance, (2) new risk-taking behaviors (e.g., smoking, driving while intoxicated, drug or alcohol abuse, irresponsible sexual behavior), (3) vague bodily complaints (e.g., headaches, stomachaches, body pains), (4) absence of future planning (e.g., inability to schedule herself to complete school projects, or to complete college applications), (5) excessive need for approval, (6) self-sacrificing (martyr) behaviors, (7) recurring nightmares, and (8) use of negative symbols (e.g., skulls, knives, dripping blood, etc. on notebooks, bedroom walls, and other personal items) (Yapko 1988).

Researchers and physicians note the difficulty in diagnosing adolescents because so many of the symptoms seem almost normal for teenagers. Nevertheless, if the above symptoms are changes from ordinary behavior, last for a long period of time, interrupt the girl's normal functioning, and do not seem to be helped by normal kinds of assistance from teachers, friends, and parents, a girl needs to be evaluated for depression. Although caregivers, obviously, do not have to make formal diagnoses, it is good for them to know what kinds of symptoms to look for to assess the depth of a girl's problem, to speak with her parents intelligently about it, and to make effective referrals to physicians or psychiatrists and counselors.

Although there is clearly no single cause for depression, there is significant evidence that girls' depression in adolescence comes with precisely the social factors described in this book. These factors, such as sexual and physical victimization, discrimination against girls in schools, and the narrow career options many girls envision for themselves, contribute to feelings of helplessness and hopelessness (Nolan-Hoeksema 1990). Depression is especially a problem for bright and high-achieving girls; girls who are intelligent are more likely to be depressed. (Boys who are intelligent are more likely *not* to be depressed.) Girls who reject sex role stereotypes are also more likely to be depressed (Block and Gjerde 1991). In addition, girls with high grade point averages in high school are more likely to be depressed (Locksley and Douvan 1979). All this suggests that girls who are intelligent, competent, and attempting to resist sex-role stereotyping are under considerable emotional stress in this culture.

There is strong evidence that girls and women also become depressed in their attempts to form and maintain intimate relationships with boys or men. Girls have often learned from their parents and other adult models that in heterosexual relationships women cannot or should not be as powerful as men. In her volume *Silencing the Self* Dana Crowley Jack analyzes interviews she conducted with twelve women who had been diagnosed as depressed by their physicians according to *DSM* (1980) guidelines. In her study she found that these women became depressed when they begin to immerse themselves in bad or unhealthy relationships. Many times they developed a sense of loss and hopelessness about the possibility of ever bringing their *own* needs and initiatives into intimate attachments. These women often talked about losing themselves in relationships with their male partners, feeling that they needed to be unauthentic (too nice or compliant) in order to keep the relationship intact. They tried hard to fulfill their partner's image of them: "I'm trying to be the way he wants me to be instead of who I am." Finally, they refrained from speaking much with their partners, because they believed they, themselves, were probably wrong (Jack 1991).

Caregiver Response

First, as with eating disorders, caregivers need to keep their eyes and ears open for signs of severe chronic depression in girls. It will often appear in conjunction with other problems, especially with eating disorders, drug and alcohol abuse, and with other symptoms of physical or sexual abuse.

Second, caregivers should speak with the parents of girls they suspect are depressed. Often parents know that something is wrong, but are unable to name what it is. This feeling causes them considerable anxiety. Visits from caregivers who are able to give them concrete information about depression may be the confirmation they need to take action to get professional attention and help for girls.

Because depression is also a symptom of some physical illnesses, an early step in getting treatment for girls who exhibit symptoms of depression is to encourage their parents to have them undergo complete physical examinations by physicians who work with and understand adolescent girls. That physicians are sympathetic to and appreciative of adolescent girls' experience is crucial. Caregivers know that girls tend to be ignored, disbelieved, and discounted by most adults. Depressed girls do not need their experience and illness minimized by physicians.

After establishing that there is no other physical cause, and after confirming the diagnosis of depression, physicians may recommend a psychiatric evaluation or may prescribe antidepressant medication. Parents are often reluctant to see their girls begin taking psychotherapeutic medication; there is still a stigma in our culture about being "mentally ill." There is also a feeling that taking medication like an antidepressant is a sign of failure or weakness. Girls, also, may be reluctant or afraid to take medications. One girl summed up her fears: "How do I know that I'll still be me, if I'm taking these pills?"

These are good questions, especially in light of the fact that girls and women have traditionally been overmedicated by the medical profession with drugs such as tranquilizers and diet pills. Two things need to be considered, however: (1) girls may not be in positions to benefit from counseling unless the symptoms of depression are alleviated, and (2) girls who are depressed are at high risk for suicide attempts. Drug treatment, monitored closely by the prescribing physicians, is sometimes a good choice, even on a short term basis. Encourage the parents and the girl to ask physicians about any concerns; they may be able to recommend books or give other reassuring information.

Antidepressant medication is not enough, however, for most girls. The stress underlying their depression is often related to social and cultural factors which will not be alleviated by antidepressants. Girls who are depressed should begin counseling with a therapist (preferably female) who can help them to replace their helpless and hopeless feelings with increased self-esteem. Therapists can also help to characterize as normal the feeling of powerlessness associated with being an adolescent girl in an androcentric culture ("Who wouldn't be depressed!").

Pastoral caregivers can also help in a girl's process of recovery. As Christie Neuger points out, depression is a psychospiritual disease often affected by and affecting a girl's relationship with the church and with God (1991, 153). The caregiver's response should not be aimed at helping a girl to feel better about her situation, which may be (and often is) truly horrible. Rather, the caregiver can give the girl three things: (1) a sense that God is *for* her and not against her; (2) realistic strategies for living and working within a cultural system that is not conducive to her growth or health; and (3) a sense of hope that her life and work can have meaning even in a hostile environment.

PROBLEMS WITH SEXUALITY

Readers will note that this section is not titled "Sexuality," but rather "Problems with Sexuality." This may seem a small point, but it signals a major issue for caregivers and adolescent girls. In our culture (and in some theology) sexuality has been equated with sexual behavior, especially intercourse, and has been labeled sinful. Many adults (Christian and other) tend to see expressions of adolescent sexuality as destructive or sinful.

In reality, sexuality is much more than intercourse. It is a part of life that all human beings share. As noted in Chapter 5, it imbues life and relationships with energy, creativity, and excitement. Like spirituality, it is at the center of who we are and how we experience the world. We are sexual beings from the moment we are born and probably from the moment our development in the womb tended toward male or female. Adolescent sexuality—for girls and boys—therefore, is a *given*, not a problem.

Certain expressions of sexuality can become problems, however, because they are *inappropriate* (i.e., sex not suitable to the situation or persons engaged in it), *unethical* (i.e., abuses of power, or relationship), *dangerous* (e.g., leading to bodily/spiritual/emotional harm), *unac-*

ceptable (i.e., outside of the accepted practice of a community) or a combination of the above.

Sexual expression for adolescents has been a problem for the church, for parents, and for themselves. Most religious traditions see sexual intercourse as appropriate only for married adults. Most parents and churches teach children and adolescents that sexuality is a gift from God. Many, however, also teach that intercourse, the act that is seen as the most complete expression of sexuality, is properly experienced only in the context of a heterosexual marriage relationship. Sexuality then is a problem because most adolescents are sexually mature by the age of thirteen or fourteen yet will not be married until their mid-twenties. What are adolescents to do during this period of approximately ten to fifteen years in which intercourse is prohibited? They must either ignore or actively reject parental and church teaching about intercourse or find other ways of expressing their sexuality.

The fact is that adolescents are sexually active in many ways before they are married: in one study 94 percent of teenagers (ages thirteen–eighteen) admitted to having erotic fantasies; 46 percent of boys and 24 percent of girls said they had masturbated. By the time adolescents get to high school they also participate in sexual behavior with partners. Approximately 47 percent of the boys and 36 percent of the girls in the study had engaged in some form of oral sex (Coles and Stokes 1985). By age eighteen, 67 percent of boys and 44 percent of girls have had sexual intercourse (National Research Council 1987). The median age for first intercourse is 16.6 years for boys and 17.4 years for girls (Alan Guttmacher Institute 1994). In the South, where adolescents are the most sexually precocious, 82 percent of adolescents have had sexual intercourse by age 19 (Janus and Janus, 1992).

For gay and lesbian teenagers, sexual behavior is even more of a problem than for heterosexual adolescents. Although the culture seems to be getting more tolerant, beliefs that homosexuality is a crime, an illness, or a sin are still common. One 1987 study found that adolescents who are openly gay faced strongly negative reactions from parents (43 percent) and friends (41 percent). They were discriminated against by peers (37 percent), verbally abused (55 percent), and physically assaulted (30 percent). Many of them had other problems, including trouble with the law, quitting school, running away from home, drug and alcohol abuse, and contracting sexually transmitted diseases (Remafedi 1987).

How does the church fit into this picture? It is clear that an adolescent's religious training has a large impact on his or her sexuality activity. Studies published in 1980 (Inazu and Fox) and 1981 (Devaney and Hubley), for example, show that an adolescent's religious beliefs have a marked influence on the age at which a boy or girl first has intercourse. Interestingly, it is not the denominational affiliation of the adolescent but the extent of commitment to a belief which seems to affect the sexual decision-making. As is probably true for most adults, the church's teachings and the individual's level of acceptance of them play a large role in decision-making. 40 percent of teenagers who are abstinent cite religious beliefs as a reason (Roper Starch Worldwide 1994).

Cargiver Response

The messages we as caregivers send adolescents are extremely important, and yet the meanings are extremely easy to get confused. What positive messages do we want to give adolescents about sexuality? At the least, theologically, we can say that (1) the body is good, and that (2) sexuality is good. God created both; human beings are constituted as bodies; we experience the world as embodied people. Too often Christian theology has split the spirit from the body, making the body a kind of prison for the spirit. Sexuality is a part of what makes us who we are; our sexuality helps us to express our love to others and our excitement for life. It is often celebrated as such in the Bible. Many times when the church talks to adolescents about sexuality, these points are missed.

Next, caregivers can tell adolescents what *we* believe about sexuality and its appropriate expression. Telling what we believe is not the same as forcing our beliefs on them. It is giving them the chance to see *how* adults think and *why*, and it gives them an opportunity to think back. The better prepared a caregiver is to explain his or her beliefs, the more benefit adolescents will receive from their testimonies. No caregiver should be reticent to say, "Sexual intercourse between young teenagers is wrong." Adolescents may disagree, but they will probably be relieved that an adult cared enough to be honest and forthright with them.

Caregivers can also help adolescents learn to make their own decisions about sexuality by discussing issues such as:

1. *spirituality.* As a gift from God, sexuality is a deeply personal expression of love. Different levels of sexual expression are appropriate for different relationships. Sexual intercourse is most appropriate for marriage or covenanted relationships.

2. *power and consent*: Persons who have substantially more power than others should never have sexual relations with those of less power, because real consent is impossible.

3. *mutuality*: All sexual relationships should be mutually agreed upon, by people mature enough to make adult decisions.

4. *fidelity*: Partners in sexual relationships should be able to trust each other to be faithful.

5. *emotional maturity*: Levels of sexual intimacy should be based on the maturity levels of the partners. Most teenagers are probably not ready to handle the emotional or spiritual consequences of an intense physical relationship.

6. *responsibility*: Sexuality entails responsibility to oneself, to one's partner, and to one's family. It has to do with safety, privacy, bodily health, and truth-telling. Some examples: (A) If one partner has a sexually transmitted disease, he or she should inform the other. (B) Not all sexual practices are safe; any practice that would harm one's own body or that of one's partner is not an expression of love. (C) Responsible sex takes planning: obtaining contraception and protection against sexually transmitted diseases requires forethought and possibly money. Boys should be as responsible as girls about this planning.

7. *sexual orientation*: Caregivers need to be knowledgeable about what sexual orientation means. About 10 percent of adolescents define themselves as primarily or exclusively attracted to others of the same gender (Boxer et al. 1993). If when we speak about sexuality with youth groups, we mention only the heterosexual orientation, we send a clear message to homosexual youth that they must remain invisible. Homosexuality can be talked about as a normal form of human sexuality. Many adolescents do not understand that harassment of gay and lesbian people is wrong. No matter what a caregiver's theological understanding of homosexuality, he or she can challenge disrespectful and harmful behaviors of this sort.

8. *risks*: About one out of ten girls in the United States becomes pregnant every year; 43 percent of all girls will have at least one pregnancy before they are 20 (Alan Guttmacher Institute 1991). 84 percent of adolescents who are abstinent list fear of pregnancy as a reason. AIDS is now the sixth leading cause of death for young people aged fifteen to twenty-four; of the reported cases of HIV infection at the end of 1991 in the United States, 31 percent were within the thirteen-to-twenty-nine age group; almost half the AIDS cases of female adolescents are due to heterosexual contact (Hein

1992). 85 percent of teenagers who say they are abstinent, list fear of sexually transmitted diseases (AIDS and others) as one of the reasons (Roper Starch Worldwide 1994). Adolescents need to be aware of the real health risks involved in sexual intercourse.

9. *alternatives*: Many teenagers have decided to wait to have sexual intercourse until they are married. One way some sex educators help adolescents think about abstinence is to have them talk about the differences between the two words: "abstinent" and "waiting." For many, "waiting" connotes something hopeful and exciting. While adolescents are waiting, they are still sexual beings. Discussions about other ways to express sexuality can be helpful.

In addition to these kinds of discussions, caregivers can sponsor sex education programs in their churches. These programs should feature training about contraceptives and sexually transmitted diseases. Music videos from MTV or other music television stations could be analyzed, along with other kinds of media portrayals of sexuality, to see what kinds of messages are being sent. The most successful programs for helping adolescents to remain abstinent seem to be those which incorporate decision-making skills with role-playing practice in saying no (Whitehead 1994).

As adults who are youth leaders or ministers, we have a responsibility to engage girls in discussions about sexuality. We should not be afraid to tell them what we believe and why; they probably want to hear this from us. Realistically, of course, we know that they will make their own decisions, and unless they are blatantly self-destructive, we should try to respect them. They will be making choices about sexuality for the rest of their lives. It is a privilege to be allowed to help them make choices on this early part of the journey.

7

RECEIVING BACK

Where there is power. . . there is also resistance. Dominant forms and institutions are continually being penetrated and reconstructed by values, styles, and knowledges that have been developing and gathering strength, energy, and distinctiveness "at the margins."

—Susan Bordo, *Unbearable Weight*

As pastoral caregivers we bring theological commitments to our work with adolescents. As religious leaders most of us have responded to the church's and God's call to nurture, train, respect, and care for those for whom we have been given responsibility. We have the best intentions toward them. We believe the church, empowered by the Holy Spirit, can be a place of healing and wholeness for individuals, families, and communities. We work hard to be people of integrity and wisdom, trustworthy and knowledgeable. We have experienced God's saving grace in our own lives, and we have a desire to share it with others, especially those in need or pain.

We also recognize the many ways we are enriched and empowered by those with whom we work and to whom we extend care. In fact, as we mature in faith and knowledge we find ourselves more aware that our relationships with parishioners or those in need are more like joint ventures or shared journeys. In Paul Tillich's words: ". . . [she] who helps in pastoral care is being helped . . . in the best act of helping, [she] is continually helping [her]self (Tillich 1984, 128).

In earlier chapters we saw how most girls learn in their families (even the best of families) that their rightful task is nurturing relationships and that their rightful place is in the private realm, away from public power. We also saw how school systems and other institutions tend to reinforce this message, how girls internalize it, and how they begin to live their lives in the underground world they create with their friends.

As pastoral caregivers we must train ourselves to resist our culture's message that girls have little of importance to offer, and we must learn to listen carefully to what girls tell us. It is a radical move to listen to a girl!

It is also a move that gives us the opportunity to hear and see a new world—a world which had heretofore been hidden from us—a world rich with ideas and insights. To help girls find their voices is also to help ourselves to tremendous resources of faith and life. From their position on the margins, or in the underground, they in some ways have a clearer view of the world than those of us ensconced in the middle do. We do not need to understand them; we can survive without them. They, in contrast, need to understand us—those who have power over them—to live. It is likely that girls know us, in some ways, better than we know ourselves.

In listening to a girl we hear our own story reflected back to us, told with a different flavor perhaps—told with caution—told with a spin only a girl could give. She may tell us truths we do not want to hear. She may trust us enough to be honest with us. There are not many resources as rich as a girl's vision.

As caregivers our calling with girls is to help them rediscover their voices; to protect them insofar as we can from violence; to encourage them to find positive ways to resist negative cultural messages; and, for our own sakes and theirs, to listen to them. When Jairus's daughter comes back to life—taking her rightful place in the world—those who stand with her will be resurrected alongside her.

APPENDIX
SPIRITUALITY QUESTIONNAIRE[1]

PERSONAL INFORMATION: Your name will *not* be mentioned in the final study. I'd like this information so I can make comparisons on specific questions, and in case I need to ask you some follow-up questions.

Name _____

Address _____

_____

Age _____

Race _____

Gender _____

Religious Affiliation (if any)_____

Phone (optional)_____

I attend formal worship services approximately _____ times per year.

PART I: Draw a picture of God on the blank piece of paper provided. (Use colors if you have pens or crayons.) Give God a name if you can. Explain your drawing and your name for God on the back of the page.

PART II: Please answer as many of these questions as you can—use the back of the page if needed. If you feel something is too personal, or not relevant just skip it. Obviously, there are no wrong or abnormal answers—**you are the expert !!!**

1. The time in my life when I felt closest to God was:
   because:
2. The most important part of my relationship with God is:
3. The feeling I get from my relationship with God is:
4. The religious figure who is most important to my faith is:
5. What I dislike most about religion is:
   because:
6. I feel God expects me to:
   because:
7. For me to please God totally I would have to:
8. I think God is closest to those who:
9. Religion is most important to me when:
10. The two most important beliefs and values in my life are:
    The most important people supporting these beliefs in my life are:
11. In my place of worship, people rarely talk about:
    I think this is because:
12. The best part about my church/synagogue/temple/mosque is:
13. My ideal way to worship is:
14. Right now I believe that after death a person:
15. The biggest problem I have with God is:
16. If I had a problem like _____ I might go to my pastor for help.
17. If I could change one thing about myself now it would be:
18. The last really important decision I made was:
    Did anyone help you to make it? _____
    If yes, what is your relationship to that person/those people? (i.e., friend, daughter, student, etc.)

    _____

19. When I think about the future _____

    _____ makes me feel the most afraid or un-happy.
20. The last time I wanted to do something that I felt I really shouldn't was:

21. I think my body is:
22. The person I most admire is:
23. My ideal life partner would be someone who:
24. My ideal friend would be someone who:
25. The one thing, above everything else, I would like to contribute to the world is:
26. (Optional) There's something else you should know about me:

PART III: Have you had an important religious experience? Please describe it briefly if you can.

Participants in the Spirituality Study
Total = 44

Ethnicity		*Religious Affiliation*	
Anglo	34	United Methodist	11
Asian	1	Church of Christ	2
Mexican American	1	Episcopal	8
African American	7	Baptist	2
Eurasian	1	Roman Catholic	6
		Greek Orthodox	1
Ages		Catholic/Jewish	1
11 years	3	Church of God (Anderson)	6
12 years	14	Presbyterian	2
13 years	1	Christian	1
14 years	3	Nondenominational	1
15 years	4	None/Don't Know	3
16 years	7		
17 years	3		
18 years	9		

NOTES

CHAPTER 1

1. Another fascinating example of this phenomenon is the original treatment twelve-year-old Anne Frank's diary received from academics in Belgium after World War II. Her diary, which has since become one of the most important documents of the war, was originally passed over in two major histories of the period because it "had seemed of small academic importance." She was mentioned, in passing, only three times in one twelve-volume work (Pappe, van der Stroom, and Barnouw 1986).

CHAPTER 2

1. Erikson has been critiqued by feminist developmentalists because he normalized autonomy and did not take full account of girls' experience in his life cycle theory. Carol Gilligan, for instance, acknowledges Erikson's contributions, especially his recognition that identity and intimacy are connected for women (Erikson 1968, 261–294), but disapproves of his not reconceptualizing his theory to include women (1982, 11–12). In an interesting critique of Gilligan's views, Donald Capps argues that Erikson can be best understood as valuing individual agency—"the exercise of one's own will"—not separateness (Capps 1995, 48–49).

CHAPTER 3

1. Caregivers should be aware, however, that even these images are not without their problems. For a critical look at the Genesis 1 story, for example, see Danna Nolan Fewell and David M. Gunn, *Gender, Power, and Promise: The Subject of the Bible's First Story*, Nashville: Abingdon Press, 1993, chapter 1.

2. See F. L. Cross and E. A. Livingston, *Oxford Dictionary of the Christian Church*, 1027.

CHAPTER 5

1. Because this chapter focuses on girls, victims will be designated "she." This usage is not in any way to suggest that boys are not victims of abuse. David Finkehor's research estimates that between 2.5 and 8.7 percent of the general

population of males have been sexually victimized as children (1984). Also, abusers are designated "he" because, although women do sexually abuse children, such abuse is believed to be extremely rare. A review of five large studies of parent-child incest revealed that the father was the offender in 97 percent of the cases (Herman 1981, 18).

2. See Adams 1994, 65–66.

3. For further information on the legal aspects of reporting child abuse see Couser, 1993.

4. See Fortune 1991, 225–233.

5. For further information on this topic see: Lebacqz and Barton 1991; Fortune 1989 and 1994.

CHAPTER 6

1. From the American Psychiatric Association: *Diagnostic and Statistical Manual of Mental Disorders*, 4th Edition. Washington, D. C.: American Psychiatric Association, 1994. Although the DSM, in its various forms, has often been inadequate (and destructive) for women, it is the reference most frequently cited by mental health professionals.

2. *DSM-IV*, 544–545.

3. *DSM-IV*, 549–550.

4. *DSM-IV*, 327.

5. *DSM-IV*, 325.

APPENDIX

1. In the design of my questionnaire, I relied heavily upon the work of both James Fowler and Anna Maria Rizzuto, pioneers in the study of faith development.

BIBLIOGRAPHY

Abraham, Suzanne and Derek Llewellyn-Jones.
    1992   *Eating Disorders: The Facts.* 3rd ed. Oxford: Oxford University Press.
Adams, Carol.
    1994   *Woman-Battering.* Minneapolis: Fortress Press.
Adams, Karen and Jennifer Fay.
    1987   *Helping Your Child Recover From Sexual Abuse.* Seattle: University of Washington Press.
Alan Guttmacher Institute.
    1994   *Sex and America's Teenagers.* Alan Guttmacher Institute quoted in *Newsweek,* October 17, 61.
American Association of University Women.
    1993   *Hostile Hallways: The AAUW Survey on Sexual Harassment in America's Schools.* Washington, D.C.
    1992   *How School Shortchanges Girls.* Washington, D.C.: American Association of University Women Foundation and National Education Association.
Apter, Terry.
    1990   *Altered Loves.* New York: St. Martin's Press.
Bem, Sandra Lipsitz.
    1993   *The Lenses of Gender.* New Haven: Yale University Press.
Bernay, T. and D. W. Cantor, ed.
    1986   *The Psychology of Today's Woman: New Psychoanalytic Visions.* Hillside, NJ: Lawrence Erlbaum.
Block, J. and P. F. Gjerde.
    1991   "Depressive Symptomatology in Late Adolescence: A Longitudinal Perspective on Personality Antecedents." In J. E. Rolf, et al., 334–360.
Bordo, Susan.
    1993   *Unbearable Weight: Feminism, Western Culture, and the Body.* Berkeley: University of California Press.

Boyd-Franklin, Nancy.
    1989   *Black Families in Therapy*. New York: Guilford Press.
Boxer, Andrew M., et al.
    1993   "Gay and Lesbian Youth." In Tolan and Cohler, 249–280.
Brown, Joanne Carlson.
    1994   "Because of the Angels: Sexual Violence and Abuse." In
            Schüssler Fiorenza and Copeland, 3–10.
Brown, Lyn Mikel.
    1993   quoted in *U.S. News and World Report*, August 2.
Brown, Lyn Mikel, and Carol Gilligan.
    1992   *Meeting at the Crossroads: Womens' Psychology and Girl's
            Development*. Cambridge, Mass.: Harvard University Press.
Bumpass, L. L.
    1984   "Children and Marital Disruption: A Replication and
            Update." *Demography* 21: 71–82.
Bureau of Justice Statistics.
    1983   *Report to the Nation on Crime and Justice: The Data*.
            Washington, D.C.: Office of Justice Programs, U.S. Dept.
            of Justice. NCJ-187068.
Capps, Donald.
    1995   *Agents of Hope: A Pastoral Psychology*. Minneapolis: For-
            tress Press.
Carter, Betty.
    1988   "Fathers and Daughters." In The Women's Project in
            Family Therapy, 90–157.
Chodorow, Nancy.
    1978   *The Reproduction of Mothering: Psychoanalysis and the Soci-
            ology of Gender*. Berkeley: University of California Press.
Chopp, Rebecca.
    1989   *The Power to Speak: Feminism, Language, God*. New York:
            Crossroad.
Cisneros, Sandra.
    1989   *The House on Mango Street*. New York: Vintage Books.
Coles, R. and G. Stokes.
    1985   *Sex and the American Teenager*. New York: Harper and Row.
Cross, F. L. and E. A. Livingstone, eds.
    1974   *Oxford Dictionary of the Christian Church*. London:
            Oxford University Press.
Couser, Richard B.
    1993   *Ministry and the American Legal System: A Guide for
            Clergy, Lay Workers, and Congregations*. Minneapolis: For-
            tress Press.

Davies, Jody Massler and Mary Gail Frawley.
  1994   *Treating the Adult Survivor of Childhood Sexual Abuse.*
          New York: Basic Books.
de Beauvoir, Simone.
  1953,   *The Second Sex.* Translated by H. M. Parshley. New York:
  1968   Knopf.
Devaney, B. L., and K. S. Hubley.
  1981   *The Determinants of Adolescent Pregnancy and Childbear-
          ing.* Washington, D.C.: Mathematica Policy Research.
DiClemente, R. J., ed.
  1992   *Adolescents and AIDS: A Generation in Jeopardy.* Newbury
          Park: Sage.
DuBois, W. E. B.
  1903   *The Souls of Black Folk.* Reprint. Greenwich, Conn: C. B. S.
          Publications, 1961.
Edelman, Marian Wright.
  1992   *The Measure of our Success.* Boston: Beacon.
Entwisle, Doris R.
  1990   "School and the Adolescent." In Feldman and Elliott,
          197–224.
Erikson, Erik.
  1959   *Identity and the Life Cycle.* New York: W. W. Norton.
  1968   *Identity: Youth and Crisis.* New York: W. W. Norton.
  1958   *Young Man Luther.* New York: W. W. Norton.
Esquire.
  1994   "*Esquire* Poll on the State of American Womanhood," 121,
          no. 2 (February):65.
Feinstein, J., et al., eds.
  1981   *Adolescent Psychiatry: Developmental and Clinical Studies.*
          vol. 9. Chicago: University of Chicago Press.
Feldman, S. Shirley and Glen R. Elliott, eds.
  1990   *At the Threshold: The Developing Adolescent.* Cambridge,
          Massachusetts: Harvard University Press.
Fewell, Danna Nolan and David M. Gunn.
  1993   *Gender, Power, and Promise: The Subject of the Bible's First
          Story.* Nashville: Abingdon.
Fine, Gary Alan, Jeylan T. Mortimer, and Donald F. Roberts.
  1990   "Leisure, Work, and the Mass Media." In Feldman and El-
          liott, 225–252.
Finkelhor, David.
  1984   *Childhood Sexual Abuse.* New York: The Free Press.

Fortune, Marie M.
   1989   *Is Nothing Sacred? When Sex Invades the Pastoral Relation-
            ship.* San Francisco: Harper and Row.
   1991   "Reporting Child Abuse: An Ethical Mandate for Ministry."
            In *Violence in the Family.* Cleveland: Pilgrim Press, 225–234.
   1994   "Clergy Misconduct: Sexual Abuse in the Ministerial Rela-
            tionship." In Schüssler Fiorenza and Copeland, 109–118.
Fuhrmann, Barbara Schneider.
   1990   *Adolescence, Adolescents.* Glenview: Scott, Foresman.
Gallers, Johanna and Kathy J. Lawrence.
   1991   "Overcoming Post-Traumatic Stress Disorder in Adoles-
            cent Date Rape Survivors." In Levy, 172–183.
Garfinkel, P. E. and D. M. Garner.
   1982   *Anorexia Nervosa: A Multidimensional Perspective.* New
            York: Brunner/Mazel.
Giarrusso, et al.
   1979   "Adolescent Cues and Signals: Sex and Sexual Assault."
            Paper presented at the Western Psychological Association
            Meeting, San Diego, Calif., April. Quoted in Parrot, 96.
Gilligan, Carol.
   1982   *In a Different Voice: Psychological Theory and Women's De-
            velopment.* Cambridge: Harvard University Press.
Gilligan, Carol, Nona P. Lyons, and Trudy J. Hanmer, eds.
   1990   *Making Connections: The Relational Worlds of Adolescent
            Girls at Emma Willard School.* Cambridge: Harvard Uni-
            versity Press.
Glaz, Maxine and Jeanne Stevenson Moessner, eds.
   1991   *Women in Travail and Transition: A New Pastoral Care.*
            Minneapolis: Fortress Press.
Glick, P. C.
   1992   "American Families: As They Are and Were" in Skolnick
            and Skolnick, 82–111.
Gomberg, E. S. and V. Franks, eds.
   1979   *Gender and Disordered Behavior.* New York: Brunner/Mazel.
Habito, Reuban L. F.
   1993   *Healing Breath: Zen Spirituality for a Wounded Earth.*
            Maryknoll, NY: Orbis Books.
Harlow, Caroline Wolf.
   1991   "Female Victims of Crime." Washington, D.C.: U.S. De-
            partment of Justice, Office of Justice Programs, Bureau of
            Justice Statistics, #91-287-P.

Hayghe, H. V.
    1990   "Family Members in the Work Force." *Monthly Labor Review*, 113:3.
Hein, K.
    1992   "Adolescents at Risk for HIV Infection." In DiClemente, 3–16.
Herman, Judith.
    1992   *Trauma and Recovery*. Cambridge: Harvard University Press.
Herman, Judith Lewis with Lisa Hirschman.
    1981   *Father-Daughter Incest*. Cambridge, Mass.: Harvard University Press.
Hetherington, E. Mavis, Tracy C. Law, and Thomas G. O'Connor.
    1993   "Divorce: Challenges, Changes, and New Chances." In Walsh, 208–234.
Hilberman, E.
    1976   *The Rape Victim*. New York: Basic Books.
Hochschild, Arlie R.
    1989   *The Second Shift: Working Parents and the Revolution at Home*. New York: Viking.
Hsu, L. K.
    1990   *Eating Disorders*. New York: The Guilford Press.
Hunter, Latoya.
    1992   *The Diary of Latoya Hunter: My First Year in Junior High*. New York: Crown Publishers.
Hutter, Mark, ed.
    1991   *The Family Experience*. New York: Macmillan.
Inazu, J. K., and G. L. Fox.
    1980   "Maternal Influence on the Sexual Behavior of Teenage Daughters." *Journal of Family Issues*, 1:81–102.
Jack, Dana Crowley.
    1991   *Silencing the Self: Women and Depression*. Cambridge, Mass.: Harvard University Press.
Janus, Mark-Davis, et al.
    1987   *Adolescent Runaways: Causes and Consequences*. Lexington, Mass.: Lexington Books.
Janus, Samuel S. and Cynthia L. Janus.
    1993   *The Janus Report of Sexual Behavior*. New York: John Wiley & Sons.
Johnson, Elizabeth A.
    1992   *She Who Is: The Mystery of God in Feminist Theological Discourse*. New York: Crossroad.

Jordan, Judith V. et al., eds.
    1991   *Women's Growth in Connection.* New York: Guilford.
Kaplan, Alexandra, Nancy Gleason, Rona Klein.
    1991   "Women's Self Development in Late Adolescence." In
            Jordan et al., 122–142.
Kaschak, Ellen.
    1992   *Engendered Lives: A New Psychology of Women's Experience.*
            New York: Basic Books.
Kashani, J. H., et al.
    1987   "Psychiatric Disorders in a Community Sample of Adoles-
            cents." *American Journal of Psychiatry,* 144:584 –589.
La Fontaine, Jean.
    1990   *Child Sexual Abuse.* Cambridge, England: Polity Press.
Laird, Joan.
    1993   "Lesbian and Gay Families." In Walsh, 282–330.
Lebacqz, Karen and Ronald G. Barton.
    1991   *Sex in the Parish.* Louisville, KY: Westminster/John Knox
            Press.
Levy, Barrie.
    1991   *Dating Violence: Young Women and Danger.* Seattle: Seal Press.
    1972   "Do Teachers Sell Girls Short?" *Today's Education,*
            61:27–29.
Lewis, C. S.
    1980   *A Grief Observed.* New York: Bantam Books.
Lewis, H. B., and J. L. Herman.
    1986   "Anger in the Mother-Daughter Relationship." In Bernay
            and Cantor, 139–163.
Locksley, A., and E. Douvan.
    1979   "Problem Behavior in Adolescents." In Gomberg and
            Franks, 71–100.
MacKinnon, Catherine.
    1987   *Feminism Unmodified.* Cambridge: Harvard University Press.
McGoldrick, Monica, John K. Pearce, and Joseph Giordano, eds.
    1982   *Ethnicity and Family Therapy.* New York: Guilford Press.
McGoldrick, Monica, Marsha Heiman, and Betty Carter.
    1993   "The Changing Family Life Cycle: A Perspective on Nor-
            malcy." In Walsh, 405–443.
Miles, Margaret.
    1994   "Textual Harassment: Desire and the Female Body." In
            Winkler and Cole, 49–63.
Morton, Nelle.
    1985   *The Journey is Home.* Boston: Beacon.

Muehlenhard, C. L., and Linton, M. A.
  1987   "Date Rape and Sexual Aggression in Dating Situations: Incidence and Risk Factors." *Journal of Counseling Psychology* 34:186–196.
Muehlenhard, C. L., and R. M. McFall.
  1981   "Dating Initiation from a Woman's Perspective." *Behavior Therapy* 12:682–91.
Myers, J. K., et al.
  1984   "Six Month Prevalence of Psychiatric Disorders in Three Communities: 1980 to 1982." *Archives of General Psychiatry* 41:959–967.
National Research Council.
  1987   *Risking the Future: Adolescent Sexuality, Pregnancy, and Childbearing.* Washington, D.C.: National Academy Press.
Neuger, Christie Cozad.
  1991   "Women's Depression: Lives at Risk." In Glaz and Moessner, 146–161.
Nolan-Hoeksema, Susan.
  1990   *Sex Differences in Depression.* Stanford, Calif.: Stanford University Press.
Orenstein, Peggy.
  1994   "Children Are Alone." *The New York Times Magazine* July 24:18–25, 32, 40, 44.
Paape, Harry, Gerrold van der Stroom, and David Barnouw.
  1986   "Introduction to *The Diary of Anne Frank*, the Critical Edition." In Hardy, H. J. J., editor. *The Diary of Anne Frank, The Critical Edition.* Prepared by the Netherlands State Institute for War Documentation. New York: Doubleday.
Parrot, Andrea.
  1992   "Why Nice Men Force Sex on Their Friends: The Problem of Acquaintance Rape." *Handbook of the Human Sexuality Program, University of Medicine and Dentistry of New Jersey—Robert Wood Johnson Medical School,* New Brunswick, NJ.
Parsons, J. E., C. M. Kaczala, and J. L. Meece.
  1982   "Socialization of Achievement Attitudes and Beliefs: Classroom Influences." *Child Development* 53:322–339.
Petzel, S. and M. Riddle.
  1981   "Adolescent Suicide: Psychosocial and Cognitive Aspects." In Feinstein, et al., 343–398.

Pirog-Good, M. A., and J. E. Stets.
  1989   *Violence in Dating Relationships: Emerging Social Issues.*
          New York: Praeger Publishers.
Procter-Smith, Marjorie.
  1990   *In Her Own Rite: Constructing Feminist Liturgical Tradi-
          tion.* Nashville: Abingdon.
Remafedi, G.
  1987   "Adolescent Sexuality: Psychosocial and Medical Implica-
          tions." *Pediatrics* 79(3):326–330.
Rich, Adrienne.
  1976   *Of Woman Born: Motherhood as Experience and Institution.*
          10th Anniversary Edition, 1986. New York: W. W. Norton.
Rizzuto, Anna Maria.
  1979   *The Birth of the Living God: A Psychoanalytic Study.* Chi-
          cago: University of Chicago Press.
Rolf, J. E., et al., eds.
  1991   *Risk and Protective Factors in the Development of Psychopa-
          thology.* New York: Cambridge University Press.
Roper Starch Worldwide.
  1994   Quoted in *Newsweek*, (Oct. 17):62.
Russell, Diana.
  1986   *The Secret Trauma.* New York: Basic Books.
Russell, Diana and Nancy Howell.
  1983   The Prevalence of Rape in the United States Revisited.
          Signs: Journal of Women in Culture and Society, 8:689.
Rutter, Peter.
  1989   *Sex in the Forbidden Zone: When Men in Power—Therapists,
          Doctors, Clergy, Teachers, and Others—Betray Women's
          Trust.* New York: Fawcett Crest.
Sadker, Myra, and David Sadker.
  1994   *Failing at Fairness: How America's Schools Cheat Girls.*
          New York: Charles Scribner's Sons.
Sadker, D., M. Sadker, and D. Thomas.
  1981   "Sex Equity and Special Education." *The Pointer*
          26:33–38.
Saussy, Carroll.
  1991   *God Images and Self Esteem: Empowering Women in a Pa-
          triarchal Society.* Louisville: Westminster/John Knox.
Schüssler Fiorenza, Elizabeth, and M. Shawn Copeland, eds.
  1994   *Violence Against Women*, Maryknoll, NY: Orbis Books.
Skolnick, Arlene S., and Jerome H. Skolnick, eds.
  1992   *Family in Transition*, 7th ed. New York: Harper Collins.

Spacks, Patricia Myers.
    1981   *The Adolescent Idea.* New York: Basic Books.
Spitzer, R. L. et al.
    1992   "A Multisite Field Trial of Diagnostic Criteria for Binge Eating Disorder." *International Journal of Eating Disorders* 11:191–203.
Stiver, Irene P.
    1991   "Beyond the Oedipus Complex." In Jordan et al., 97–121.
Striegel-Moore, R. H., L. R. Silberstein, and J. Rodin.
    1986   "Toward an Understanding of Risk Factors in Bulimia." *American Psychologist* 41: 246–264.
Sugarman, David B., and Hotaling, Gerald T.
    1989   "Dating Violence: Prevalence, Context, and Risk Markers." In Pirog-Good and Stets, 3–32.
Tavris, Carol.
    1992   *The Mismeasurement of Woman: Why Women Are Not the Better Sex, the Inferior Sex, or the Opposite Sex.* New York: Simon & Schuster.
Tillich, Paul.
    1984   *The Meaning of Health: Essays in Existentialism, Psychoanalysis, and Religion,* ed. Perry LeFevre. Chicago: Exploration Press.
Tolan, Patrick H. and Bertram J. Cohler, eds.
    1993   *Handbook of Clinical Research and Practice with Adolescents.* New York: John Wiley & Sons, Inc.
U. S. Justice Department.
    1995   The National Crime Victimization Survey, Redesigned, August, 1995.
    1994   Statistics reported in *The Dallas Morning News,* June 23:8a.
Visher, Emily B., and John S. Visher.
    1993   "Remarriage Families and Stepparenting." In Walsh, 235–253.
Walsh, Froma, ed.
    1993   *Normal Family Processes.* 2nd ed., New York: Guilford Press.
Ward, Janie Victoria.
    1990   "Racial Identity Formation and Transformations." In Gilligan, Lyons, and Hanmer, 215–232.
Weitzman, Lenore.
    1991   "Divorce and the Illusion of Equality." In Hutter, 243–280.

Whitehead, Barbara Dafoe.
      1994   "The Failure of Sex Education." *Atlantic Monthly*, Octo-
              ber, 55–80.
Wider Opportunities for Women Survey.
      1993   Quoted in *The Dallas Morning News*, April 29:C1.
Winkler, Mary G., and Letha B. Cole, eds.
      1994   *The Good Body: Asceticism in Contemporary Culture.* New
              Haven: Yale University Press.
"Women Work!"
      1994   Quoted in *U.S. News and World Report*, March 28:50.
The Women's Project in Family Therapy.
      1988   *The Invisible Web: Gender Patterns in Family Relationships.*
              New York: Guilford.
Woodman, Marion.
      1980   *The Owl Was a Baker's Daughter: Obesity, Anorexia Ner-
              vosa, and the Repressed Feminine.* Toronto: Inner City
              Books.
Wyatt, Gail.
      1985   "The Sexual Abuse of Afro-American and White Women in
              Childhood." *Child Abuse and Neglect* 9:507–519.
Yapko, M. D.
      1988   *When Living Hurts: Directives for Treating Depression.*
              New York: Brunner/Mazel.